Y0-DWP-183

Also available from Northwest Parent Publishing, Inc.:

Monthly Newsmagazines for Parents
Eastside Parent
Pierce County Parent
Portland Parent
Seattle's Child

Books
For Families and Friends Coupon Book
Going Places: Family Getaways in the Pacific Northwest
The Mudpies Activity Book: Recipes for Invention

The Ultimate Guide for Fun and Learning Around Puget Sound

By Ann Bergman and
Colleen Carroll

Edited by
Meaghan McGavick Dowling

First Edition

Northwest Parent Publishing, Inc.
Seattle, Washington

Thanks to our families and co-workers, who hardly recognize us anymore, and to Susan Bureau for her keen eye.

Printed in the United States of America.

Northwest Parent Publishing, Inc.
2107 Elliott Avenue, Suite 303
Seattle, Washington 98121 U.S.A.
(206) 441-0191

IBSN: 0–9614626–3–9

Art direction by Simon Sung

Design, layout and production by
Nita Brautlacht and Simon Sung

Acknowledgments/Credits

P. 95, from A Field Guide to Seattle's Public Art. Copyright 1991, Seattle Arts Commission and reprinted by permission.

Who we are.

We are editors for Northwest Parent Publishing, a company that publishes four award-winning parenting newsmagazines in the Northwest: *Seattle's Child, Eastside Parent, Pierce County Parent* and *Portland Parent.*

More importantly, we are parents raising our kids in the Seattle area, who share a mission to provide other parents with reliable information so they can make good decisions and get the most out of family time.

Why we needed this book.

We love our kids and we love Seattle. We needed to know what this city could offer our kids, day to day, season by season, year-round. We wanted to know what bike trails are suitable for wobbly riders, what facilities offer family memberships, what to do when the kids start bouncing off the walls in the middle of winter or summer vacation. Simply stated, we needed one source to help us see this incredible city from a *parent's* perspective. Adults have many excellent guides to help them explore Seattle; parents have few—none of which is as candid and comprehensive as this.

How we wrote this book.

We walked, rode, visited, asked, discussed and ate. We researched, compiled, double-checked, edited, added. We talked with our friends, our parents, our children and strangers.

Because of our monthly parenting publications, we had much to start with in our own offices: volumes of calendar and event listings, articles about programs and facilities for children, and all the news about current kid-oriented plans and projects. We sifted out the mediocre and kept our standards high in putting together a list of recommended places to go and things to do with kids in Seattle. And though we lost a few nights of sleep in the process, we feel we've published an indispensable guide book for both residents and tourists—one that we, ourselves, wouldn't be caught without.

How to use this book.

The listings in *Out and About Seattle with Kids* were current at press time, but we urge you to confirm hours, prices and locations of selected destinations.

We used three icons throughout this guide:

Offers classes and/or workshops for children

Offers field trips for schools or small groups

Offers birthday party packages

We also included ***Tips*** and ***Essentials*** with some entries (which could just as easily have been termed "unsolicited advice" and "hard-learned facts").

See also the quick index on page 203 for fun outing suggestions.

TABLE OF CONTENTS

CHAPTER 1

Animals, Animals, Animals

Some of us can remember going to the zoo as children and seeing mostly cement and bars, pits and cages. It seems sad and barren in retrospect, but few of us paid attention to those factors then. Instead, we stood on our tippy toes or sat on our fathers' shoulders, trying to catch a glimpse of the animals. And when we did, we didn't think about how great it would be if they were free to roam their homelands; we thought about how much we'd like to have monkeys as pets or how weird-looking ostriches were.

Kids still look at the monkeys and want to take them home. But the zoos that they visit, at least in this neck of the woods, are dramatically different from the ones we might remember. "Natural" habitats have been created and animals roam freer (excepting the snakes and creepy critters—thank goodness).

If your kids need a change of scenery from the usual lions, tigers and bears, take them off to one of the fine aquariums in the area, or visit some good old barnyard friends at a local petting farm.

Kelsey Creek Community Park/Farm

13204 SE 8th Place, Bellevue
455-7688
Park open dawn to dusk year-round; public viewing of animals, 8 am-4 pm daily
Free admission; free parking
Directions: Take Exit 12 (SE 8th Street) from I-405 and go east on SE 8th. Follow this road through the intersection at Lake Hills Connector to the stop sign at 128th Ave SE and turn left; follow 128th to SE 4th Place and turn right. Kelsey Creek Park is just ahead.

If someone in your family either loves or doesn't recognize rabbits, chickens, horses, cows, goats, donkeys and pigs, this farm-in-the-city is well worth a visit. Farm in this case means a lovely, big red barn and adjacent small buildings that house the usual assortment of farm animals. Behind the barn are corrals for the horses, and next to the barn is a first-class playground for the kids. Kids can wander through the barn at their own pace, enjoying up-close views of their favorite farm animals. This 80-acre expanse also has a creek, trails and plenty of open lawns, so take a picnic and enjoy the setting.

☆ Tips

Spring brings the arrival of many baby animals to Kelsey Creek. If you want to give your child a chance to watch a birthing scene or see some new babies, call in early spring to find out the EDTs (Expected Delivery Times) of the pregnant animals.

Other special events include the Farm Fair in early November and sheep shearing in mid-March.

☆ Essentials

The barn is about five minutes from the parking area and accessible by stroller, though toddlers can easily handle the walk.

Restroom facilities are available near the parking area but not at the barn. No food or drink is sold at the park, so bring your own.

Nearby attractions: Bellefield Nature Park, Bellevue Art Museum, Rosalie Whyel Museum of Doll Art.

Northwest Trek Wildlife Park

11610 Trek Dr E, Eatonville; 17 miles south of Puyallup
1-800-433-TREK
Open year-round; seasonal hours vary
$7.50/adults; $6.50/seniors; $5/ children 5-17 years; $3/children 3-4 years; children 2 & under free;
Annual membership: $45/family
Directions: Take Exit 142B from I-5 and travel south on State Route 161. Northwest Trek is 17 miles south of Puyallup on SR 161. About 55 miles from Seattle; 35 miles from Tacoma.

In 1971, Dr. and Mrs. David T. Hellyer donated 600 acres of beautiful forest, lake and meadow land to the Metropolitan Park District of Tacoma to create a protected place where Northwest wildlife could roam free. The result of their generosity is a unique park ideally suited to children. Tram tours led by expert naturalists depart hourly, taking visitors throughout 435 acres of free-roaming habitat, which is home to bison, bighorn sheep, elk, caribou, water fowl, moose, mountain goat, blacktail deer and many others. Don't be surprised to see a curious caribou walking alongside the tram or a herd of bison calmly grazing in the thicket—so close that your child can almost reach out and pat their heads!

The naturalist guides provide plenty of interesting information about the behavior of these magnificent animals, which will hold the attention of most school-age kids. Preschoolers are typically thrilled by the tram ride at least as much as by seeing the animals.

The walk-through area is a network of paved pathways, easily negotiated by wheelchairs or strollers, which allows children close-up views of raccoons, beavers, badgers, lynx, bobcat, cougars and wolves. Informative signs explain the habitat of these Northwest natives, as well as the plight of the many endangered species.

At the Cheney Discovery Center, a cabin designed specifically for hands-on activities, kids can hold frogs and garter snakes, examine the differences in animal fur coats, and explore habitats and characteristics of many Northwest wildlife.

> ☆ ***Tips***
>
> *Try to allow at least three hours to take in all the activities at Northwest Trek: the one-hour tram tour, hands-on activities at the Discovery Center, a visit to the walk-through area, browsing in the gift shop and lunch in the cafe.*
>
> *The gift shop is exceptionally good; you might want to encourage the kids to bring some spending money for a souvenir.*

Photo credit: Northwest Trek

At Northwest Trek your child will get an up-close look at native wildlife.

☆ *Essentials*

Parking is free. Strollers are *not* available for rent. Strollers/back-packs are advised to get from the parking area—a short walk on level, paved pathways. Northwest Trek features over five miles of hiking trails through wooded areas, as well as a paved 3/4-mile loop easily accessible to strollers and wheel-chairs. A changing table is located in the women's restroom. Guides to native plant life are available at the trail entrance and the office. There are plenty of tables for picnicking. The cafe offers dining inside or out; on chilly days you can warm your-self by the fireplace. The food is basic (burgers, chicken sandwiches, etc.), tasty and reasonably priced.

Nearby attractions: Pioneer Farm in Eatonville.

Point Defiance Park, Zoo & Aquarium

5400 North Pearl Street, Tacoma
591-5335
Open daily year-round except Thanksgiving Day and Christmas Day. Open Labor Day-Memorial Day, 10 am-4 pm; Memorial Day-Labor Day, 10 am-7 pm
Admission to the park grounds is free. Zoo & Aquarium admission: $6.25/adult; $5.75/seniors & disabled adults; $4.50/children 5-17 years; $2.25/children 3-4 years; children 2 & under free
Annual membership: $45/family
Directions: From I-5 take Exit 132, follow signs to Hwy 16. Take a left on the 6th Ave exit from Hwy 16, take a right on Pearl St and follow the signs to Point Defiance Park, Zoo & Aquarium.

Don't go to Point Defiance Park, Zoo & Aquarium expecting to see and do everything in one visit; you can't possibly experience all it has to offer in one day. Owned and

☆ ***Tips***

Each December, Zoolights transforms Point Defiance Zoo & Aquarium into a fantasy land of over 450,000 lights, covering pathways, trees and buildings, and creating over 100 illuminated animals, nursery rhyme characters and local landmarks. Try to visit Zoolights early in December, as this attraction gets busy later in the month.

During the spring and summer months, the Zoo & Aquarium hosts ZooSnoozes for children of all ages. These overnight "camp-outs" include activities designed to teach children about animals who make the sea their home.

operated by the Metropolitan Park District of Tacoma, Point Defiance Park is the second largest city park in the United States (first is Central Park, and if you've ever been lucky enough to take a taxi through that place, you know it's *big*).

About an hour's drive from Seattle, Point Defiance covers 698 acres, and comprises the Zoo & Aquarium, Never Never Land, Fort Nisqually (a restored Hudson Bay Company fort) and the Camp 6 Logging Museum. The park terrain consists of scenic floral gardens, old growth forests, playgrounds, tennis courts and superb picnic areas featuring grills, electricity, water and covered shelters. There are beaches as well, where you can rent boats, fish, swim or sunbathe.

On Saturday mornings, the park's wooded Five-Mile Drive is closed to automobile traffic until 1 pm, making it a good time to take the kids for a stroll or bike ride.

Point Defiance Zoo & Aquarium, also known as The Pacific Rim Zoo due to its focus on animals from countries bordering the Pacific Ocean, houses more than 5,000 animals within its 29 acres. It's not uncommon to see baby beluga whales playing catch, penguins playing and nesting, or polar bears swimming underwater. A popular stop for children is the farm, where they can pet goats, cows, sheep, rabbits and llamas. A quarter buys a handful of food to feed some of these friendly residents—a real thrill for little city slickers.

The Zoo & Aquarium complex features both over- and underwater

views of polar bears, beluga whales, walruses, seals, sea otters and sea lions, as well as exhibits showcasing species ranging from the massive African and Asian elephants (you can even take a ride!) to small mammals, birds and reptiles. The recently renovated Simpson Marine Discovery Lab offers hands-on activities designed to focus on the water quality of Puget Sound.

The popular North Pacific Aquarium and side exhibits feature marine life in the cold-water regions of the Pacific Northwest, including the playful sea otters, octopi, wolf eel and other species native to this area. The Discovery Reef Aquarium illustrates life in warm waters and is home to sharks and dozens of colorful tropical fish. Watch out! Your two-year-old may not like being face-to-face with a huge shark!

If your kids are suffering a reality overdose, take them into Never Never Land, a children's storyland featuring a 10-acre forest full of 41 life-size characters from favorite children's literature, including Peter Rabbit, Humpty Dumpty, Hansel and Gretel, and Goldilocks and the Three Bears. Never Never Land is open March through September—weekends only in March, April and September and daily May through August. Admission is $2/adults, $1.50/teens & seniors; $1/children 3-12; children 2 & under are free. Group tours and birthday parties are welcome by reservation; call 591-5845.

Fort Nisqually is a restored Hudson Bay Company fort complete with a working blacksmith shop and several restored buildings, as well as a unique gift shop featuring pottery and other souvenirs. The best time to visit is Wednesday through Sunday between Memorial Day and Labor Day, when all the historic buildings are open for viewing. Summer admission is $1/adults and $.50/children (admission is free during the remainder of the year, but the historical buildings are not always open); call ahead to confirm hours of operation, 591-5339.

Camp 6 offers authentic steam locomotive rides for a small fee beginning each year in April. A special Santa Train runs each December; call 752-0047 for more information.

☆ *Essentials*

Parking is free and located conveniently adjacent to the Zoo & Aquarium; stroller rentals are available on a first-come, first-served basis for $3. Maps are available at the entrance to Point Defiance or you can call ahead to receive one by mail, 591-5335. The two gift shops—one at the main gate, the other in the aquarium—feature a good assortment of souvenirs and gift ideas. Bring a picnic, grab a snack at one of the snack bars located throughout the park grounds, or order lunch in the cafe at the zoo. The cafe prices are reasonable (about $2-$3 for a hamburger) and the food is quite good.

the seattle aquarium

Seattle Aquarium & Omnidome

Pier 59, Waterfront Park, Seattle Aquarium 386-4320, Omnidome 622-1868
Aquarium is open year-round; Labor Day-Memorial Day, 10 am-5 pm; Memorial Day-Labor Day, 10 am-7 pm
Aquarium admission: $6.50/adults; $5/seniors & disabled adults; $4/ children ages 6-18 years; $1.50/ children 3-5 years; children 2 & under are free
Admission to Omnidome & Aquarium: $10.75/adults; $6.75/ children 13-18 & seniors; $5.75/ children 6-12; $4.30/children 3-5; children 2 & under are free
Annual Aquarium Membership: $40/family

The Seattle Waterfront offers a wide variety of attractions for the entire family, but the Seattle Aquarium has to be one of the best. Set right over the water on Pier 59, the Aquarium's view of Elliott Bay features a variety of vessels, including ferries, container ships and tug boats. The Aquarium offers a beautiful trip beneath the waters of Puget Sound and around the world.

Entering the Aquarium is a breathtaking escape into a world of color and movement. The lights are dimmed, setting off the colors from within the many lighted tanks. Informative descriptions of the exhibits are located throughout the aquarium, if you can get the kids to stop long enough to read them!

Your first stop within the aquarium is the Principles of Survival exhibit, which features beautiful seahorses, leaffish and lionfish, followed by a favorite of the kids, the Local Invertebrates exhibit and a giant Pacific octopus. Next, a special exhibit showcases aquatic animals from the waters of Japan in the exhibit Suizoku: Water Beings. Restrooms are located just beyond the Suizoku exhibit; when you pass them, look up and see a model of a great white shark hanging overhead (Puget Sound is home to seven kinds of sharks). Watch black-tipped reef sharks lurking and darting in the Pacific Coral Reef exhibit, and see interesting tropical crabs that can even crack coconuts in the Coconut Crab exhibit. Kids can touch starfish and other creatures outside in the Touch Tank, and watch diving birds in the Birds and Shores

☆ *Tips*

The Seattle Aquarium is a good "first outing" for an infant in a backpack—the bright fish colors are captivating. Visitor's maps are free and offer an excellent overview of the featured exhibits. Allow some time for browsing in the Sandpiper Gift and Book Store, which you will enter as you exit the exhibit area; keep your Aquarium receipt in order to leave and re-enter the Aquarium.

See In & Around Downtown/ Seattle Waterfront for information about other places of interest to visit on the waterfront.

exhibit. (Feeding time for the diving birds is approximately 11 am, daily.)

The Seattle Aquarium offers the only aquarium-based salmon run in the world, featuring a fish ladder and interesting information about the migration of these fascinating creatures. (Late summer and early fall are the best viewing times.)

One of the most popular features of the Aquarium is the 400,000-gallon Underwater Dome, a glassed-in area where families can observe life under the sea. Even an infant will be mesmerized by the action in this "inside-out" aquarium. If you schedule your visit at about 1:30 pm, you'll witness the aquarium's divers feeding the dome residents. (This spectacular room can be rented for private parties when the Aquarium is closed.)

Up from the dome is the open-air Otters and Seals exhibit, where playful sea otters twirl and romp. This is followed by the Delicate Balance exhibit, which teaches visitors about the politics and pollution affecting Puget Sound. This is primarily printed information, although there are some interesting displays and hands-on activities that even young children may enjoy.

Adjacent to the Aquarium is the Omnidome Theatre, featuring films that put you so close to the action, you feel you are a part of it. Whether it's a ride in a helicopter viewing the destruction of Mount St. Helens or a trip above the earth with the Canadian Air Force, these movies offer breathtaking footage with entertaining and informative narrative. Warning: While these movies are typically a great hit with ages five and up, younger kids may be frightened and overwhelmed by the huge screen.

Length of each film is about 45 minutes; admission can be purchased for the Omnidome only ($5.95/adults; $4.95/ages 13-18 & seniors; $3.95/ages 3-12; under 3 are free), or in combination with admission to the Aquarium (see above).

☆ *Essentials*

Parking is available across the street from the Aquarium using either meters or the Public Market parking garage. (Stock up on quarters if you use the meters, six quarters buys you just 1 1/2 hours).

The garage costs $4 for 2-3 hours of parking. Metro buses don't run along the waterfront, but the Waterfront Trolley travels between the International District and Pier 70, with several stops along Alaskan Way. Adult fares are: non-rush hour, $.85; rush-hour, $1.10. Child fare is $.75 at all times.

Stroller rentals are usually available at the Aquarium, but call ahead to be sure they are in service. Aisles and ramps are easily accessible to strollers and wheelchairs. Some exhibits, such as the Touch Tank, are outdoors, so dress for the weather.

King County residents with proof of residency receive admission discounts. Joint annual memberships for the Seattle Aquarium and Woodland Park Zoo are available for $68.

Steamers, a tasty fish and chip spot, is located right outside the Aquarium. Just south at the Bay Pavilon on Pier 57 there are several places to snack. On the Hillclimb—the stairs leading to the Pike Place Market—you'll find El Puerco Lloron, a very good, inexpensive Mexican restaurant.

Nearby attractions: See In & Around Downtown/Seattle Waterfront for other waterfront attractions.
Across the street from the north entrance to the Aquarium, you'll find steep stairs (aptly called the Hillclimb) leading to the Pike Place Market. See In & Around Downtown/Hillclimb and In & Around Downtown/Pike Place Market.

Washington Zoological Park

5410 194th Ave SE, Issaquah; just south of I-90
391-5508
Open year-round Tues-Sun; Apr-Sept: Tues-Sat, 10 am-5 pm, Sun, 11 am-5 pm; Oct-Mar: Tues-Sat, 10 am-4 pm, Sun, 11 am-4 pm. Closed Thanksgiving Day, Dec 24, 25, 26 & 31, & Jan 1
Admission: $2-$4; children under 2 free
Annual membership: $36/family
Directions: Take Exit 15 from I-90 and go south on the Renton-Issaquah Rd. Turn right onto Newport Way and travel west to SE 54th. Follow 54th up the hill to the zoo.

Washington Zoological Park is a community service teaching facility, which offers visitors a different look into the wild kingdom. Established in 1972 by Cougar Mountain Academy, this 14-acre zoo specializes in threatened or endangered animals and birds, and is currently home to such creatures as emus, parrots, cockatoos, cranes, reindeer and cougars.

The Washington Zoological Park is relatively small and intimate, allowing kids to observe these magnificent creatures up-close. Visitors can walk through the zoo at their own pace or take a guided tour; experienced volunteer docents will answer questions about the many animals. During school field trips docents will often take a cougar out of its cage to give the kids a rare close encounter.

☆ Essentials

No food is sold at the park and there are no picnic areas. The free parking lot is conveniently located adjacent to the entrance. Negotiating a stroller through the zoo is tricky, so backpacks are advised whenever possible. A walk through the zoo can easily be accomplished by even the youngest visitor.

Nearby attractions: All For Kids Books & Music in Issaquah, the Herbfarm, Lake Sammamish State Park.

☆ Tips

Wolf Haven community programs include Adopt-a-Wolf, which offers individuals an opportunity to have a direct impact on the life of a wolf, and Howl-Ins, special Friday night events held May through September, which feature a tour of the park, master storytellers, sing-alongs, marshmallow roasts and howling with the wolves around the campfire.

Wolf Haven International

3111 Offut Lake Rd, Tenino; about 10 miles south of Olympia
264-4695
Open daily May-Sept, 10 am-5 pm; open Wed-Sun, Oct-Apr, 10 am-4 pm
$5/adults; $2.50/children 6-12 years; children under 6 are free
Annual membership tax-deductible: $50/family
Directions: About 10 miles south of Olympia, take Exit 99 from I-5 and go east onto 93rd St. Follow 93rd to Old Hwy 99 and turn right. Go 3 1/2 miles south and turn left onto Offut Lake Rd. Wolf Haven is just 1/4 mile ahead.

Wolf Haven International, a non-profit organization, was established in 1982 to study, care for and preserve an animal on the verge of extinction. Hunting, poisoning, trapping and habitat destruction have led to the near disappearance of the wolf, and Wolf Haven is actively working to stop this trend. Wolf Haven is currently home to about 36 wolves of various subspecies. In addition to guided tours of the 65-acre sanctuary, Wolf Haven offers outreach programs to schools, civic organizations and others within the community, dedicated to educating the public about the importance of wildlife.

Woodland Park Zoo

5500 Phinney Ave N, Seattle
684-4800
Opens daily at 9:30 am year-round; closing time varies with the season
$6/adults;$4.50/seniors & disabled adults; $3.50/children 6-17 years; $1.50/children 3-5 years; ages 2 & under free
Annual membership: $39/family
Directions: Take Exit 169 from I-5 (N 50th St). Go west on N 50th about 1 1/3 miles to the south gate of the zoo, located at the intersection of N 50th & Fremont Ave.

The Tropical Rain Forest exhibit is home to over 50 different animals and nearly 700 plant species.

Rated one of the 10 best zoos in the United States, the Woodland Park Zoo is an outstanding example of what a zoo can be—if the time and money are spent to recreate natural habitats where the animals roam free. Conveniently located just 10 minutes from downtown Seattle, the 92-acre zoo features an extensive array of animals, many in wide open areas, not cramped cages. Giraffes, zebras and hippos roam within the African Savannah exhibit; elephants plod through the Asian Elephant exhibit; gorillas go native in their jungle home. The new Tropical Rain Forest (opened in September 1992) makes a vivid impression with an exhibit that takes visitors from the floor of the forest high up into the canopy.

One of the favorite exhibits for children is the Nocturnal House where bats, raccoons, lizards and others demonstrate their rituals in a nighttime environment. It is linked to the Reptile House, which is equally popular with kids, and likely to get a few oohs, ahhs and eeks. Strollers must be left outside both these exhibits.

The popular Family Farm, where children are allowed to touch the animals, has been closed to allow for construction of the new Temperate Forest, which will encompass the Family Farm and is scheduled to be completed in spring 1994.

The new Family Farm will emphasize the agricultural practices of the Northwest and provide opportunities to observe and participate in basic activities that take place on a small working farm.

Along the Habitat Discovery Trail, children will be able to explore larger than life-size animals' homes. Using their imaginations, they can turn themselves into orb-weaving spiders as they climb giant spider webs, river otters as they slide down otter slides or moles as they squirm through a simulated mole burrow.

In the Farm's Reflection Center,

☆ *Tips*

Woodland Park Zoo is a fabulous place to take a child for an outing. If you live in the area, consider investing in a family pass so you'll feel free to make unlimited visits. A leisurely zoo outing on a cloudy winter day is an altogether different experience than a trip to the zoo on a hot, crowded weekend in the summer.

The Education Center, located by the west entry to the zoo, is open every day, 8:30 am-5 pm. Visitors can stop by to pick up informational brochures, participate in educational programs, or explore the Discovery Room (weekends only), offering young visitors a variety of hands-on experiences.

Pony rides are offered in the northwest corner of the zoo daily during the summer months. The hours are limited, usually 11 am-3 pm, and the cost is $1.50. Children must be at least two years of age; the maximum weight is 120 pounds. There is often a line, and the rider is led just once around the corral, but this is a big thrill and very popular, especially with very young children (someone walks alongside to be sure they stay on).

The zoo presents an outdoor summer concert series during July and August on the North Meadow. These evening concerts are free for kids 12 and under when accompanied by an adult. Call the zoo for more information, 684-4800.

kids will be able to magnify bugs through a bioscanner and use interactive computer stations to learn about the natural environment of the Pacific Northwest.

☆ *Essentials*

Parking is available in lots next to the north and south entrances to the zoo; cost is $2 for four hours. Wheelchair and stroller rentals are available on a first-come, first-served basis beginning at 10 am for $1.75 from the ZooStore next to the south gate. Bring a picnic lunch or stop by the many concession stands offering hot dogs, soft drinks, popcorn and other goodies. King County residents with proof of residency receive admission discounts. Joint annual memberships for the Seattle Aquarium and Woodland Park Zoo are available for $68.

Nearby attractions: Green Lake, Hiram M. Chittenden Government Locks, Woodland Park.

CHAPTER 2

Harvests

In the urban world of 24-hour grocery stores and we-have-everything warehouses, it is easy for a child to forget about the real source of food and plants: land. And though the appeal of being able to buy your food, pumpkins and even Christmas trees at your local supermarket is undeniable, so is the experience of going out to the farms where they come from, and allowing your kids to pick and choose for themselves.

Luckily, you don't have to drive too far to get back to nature, and the minute you are out of city traffic, you'll be glad you made the effort. The sweet fragrance of a strawberry field, the cool frost on a pumpkin patch, the brays and nays of farm animals—you're likely to get caught up in the romance of it all, and the entire family will be better off for a bit of country air.

Berry Picking

Just about the time summer vacation begins, ripe strawberries, raspberries and blueberries are ready for picking. Boxes are usually supplied at u-pick farms; you and your kids just wander among the fields and pick to your hearts' content. When finished, your berries are weighed and you pay by the pound. No reservations are necessary, but try to go early in the day when the selection is best. Many vines become pretty bare by the end of the day. It's hard work, but the rewards are immediate!

Each year *The Farm Fresh Guide* is published in April, listing names, addresses, crops and hours of operation for many of the u-pick farms throughout King, Pierce, Skagit, Snohomish and Thurston counties. The guide is available free at public libraries and Chamber of Commerce offices beginning in April or May, or you may send a $.29 stamp along with a self-addressed label to: Sue Kinser, Puget Sound Farm Markets Assoc., 1733 NE 20th Street, Renton, WA 98056.

☆ ***Tips***

When berry picking, use sunscreen and hats for sun protection, and bring food and plenty of drinks. Also, show the kids how to maneuver between the rows of plants carefully. Make sure they understand which berries are ripe for picking (there are little secrets the farmer might share), and don't pick more than your family can eat or process in a few days, because berries spoil quickly.

Fruit Rolls

If you have a food dehydrator and enough extra berries, try this quick and easy recipe:

2 cups of fresh fruit
1 T. lemon juice
1/4 cup water

Pull a chair up to the counter and allow your kids to mix these ingredients in the blender. Then pour the mixture into the drying trays. After the fruit dries, get the kids to roll it up and wrap with plastic. Seal with a sticker!

—Sue Jackson

Pumpkin Harvests

Just when the fallen leaves have been drained of their last vestiges of color and the dreary drizzle of autumn has settled in, Halloween comes along and rejuvenates our spirits (quite literally, according to some). Children adore this holiday—creating fun costumes, trick-or-treating and, of course, carving their jack-o'-lanterns for display on the window or porch.

Many pumpkin farms offer an array of special activities throughout October, including hay rides, haunted houses, scarecrows and costumed characters. Call ahead to confirm hours of operation and to verify special events, since they're apt to change from year to year.

Photo credit: Roberta Wilkes

Tasty Pumpkin Seeds

Once you have scooped the insides out of the pumpkins, rinse the seeds thoroughly (or boil them), spread them on a baking sheet, and coat them with butter and any of the following: paprika, garlic, salt or seasoning salt. Bake at 425° for 15-20 minutes (stirring them a few times) until golden brown and crisp. Optional: sprinkle with parmesan cheese.

Aqua Barn Ranch

15227 SE Renton-Maple Valley Hwy, Renton
255-4618

Offers Pumpkin Patch Parties for children ages eight and under, featuring hay rides, farm animals, pumpkin harvesting and an array of special activities. Reservations are required.

Baylor Farm

28511 Ben Howard Rd, Monroe
793-0822

Offers tractor rides, farm animals, pumpkin displays and harvesting. Groups are welcome during the week by reservation; open to the public on weekends.

Biringer Farm

Near Marysville; just north of Everett on I-5
259-0255

Features wagon rides that take children and families to the pumpkin patches. Call ahead to confirm hours and event schedule.

Country Pickin's
Country Village, 23804 Bothell-Everett Hwy, Bothell
485-0191

A suburban pumpkin patch for those who prefer to avoid the mud! Attractions include a barnyard with live scarecrows, hot apple cider and farm animals. No group tours are offered; open daily to the public.

Craven Farm
13817 Shorts School Rd, Snohomish
568-2601

Offers a special event each year for preschool and elementary school children. Attractions include a live pumpkin who greets the children and tells them a story about the farm, a friendly witch who introduces the kids to the farm animals, and pumpkin harvesting right from the vine. Reservations are required weekdays; drop-in on weekends. A nominal fee (about $3/child) includes the tour, a cookie and a pumpkin; adults are free.

☆ Tips

At many of these farms, pumpkins have already been cut from the vine and are lying free in the fields, so if cutting your own is of particular importance, be sure to call ahead to verify that feature. The cost of the pumpkins varies from farm to farm but is usually determined individually by weight. Remember to dress warmly, wear your boots and bring the camera!

Farmer Dan's
26634 SE 196th, Hobart; southeast of Issaquah
432-1705

Fun for the entire family includes scarecrows made by school children, farm animals, hot cider and hot chocolate, and a hay barn. Group tours are scheduled on weekdays; the public is welcome select hours during the week and all day Saturday and Sunday.

Hands-On Pumpkin Farm
15308 52nd Ave W, Edmonds
743-3694

Offers educational field trips for all ages. Children are led on a 40-minute tour of the farm, which includes time to pet and feed some of the animals before picking pumpkins. Reservations are required. Special rates apply; adults are free with school groups.

The Herbfarm
32804 Issaquah-Fall City Rd, Fall City
784-2222

Offers storytelling, scarecrows, a hay maze and the Great Pumpkin. Weekdays by appointment; drop-in on Saturdays and Sundays. Flat rates apply (about $5/person), which include activities and a pumpkin.

Remlinger Farms
32610 NE 32nd St, Carnation
451-8740

An authentic working farm operated year-round. Covered-wagon rides, a hay maze, barnyard animals, special events, storytelling and exhibits are all part of the fun. Weekdays by appointment; drop-in on Saturdays and Sundays.

Top of the Hill Pumpkin Patch
16533 36th Ave W, Alderwood Manor
743-4250

This is *not* a u-pick patch; pumpkins are already picked and ready for purchase. Attractions include scarecrow people and farm animals. Reservations required for groups; individuals welcome anytime.

Christmas Tree Farms

Bundle up the family and visit one of the area's Christmas tree farms for a special outing during the winter holidays. Many farms offer hot cider, coffee and holiday goodies, as well as special attractions such as tractor rides and Santa. Each year, the Puget Sound Christmas Tree Association, Inc. publishes a guide listing its member Christmas tree farms, including addresses, phone numbers and hours of operation for each farm, as well as any special amenities. This free guide is available during November and December at Chamber of Commerce offices and public libraries throughout the Puget Sound area. The Northwest Christmas Tree Association also publishes a guide covering Washington and Oregon, which is available locally during the holidays. Call (503) 364-2942 to receive a free copy or for more information.

Aunt Stina's Pepparkakor

This Scandinavian recipe is especial[ly] popular with kids because the final product can either be eaten or hung on the tree (or both) and the cookies are very tasty. It will yield enough cookies to trim a small tree and can be doubled successfully. The dough keeps well in the freezer, if you want to plan ahead.

Combine
1/2 lb. butter or margarine (2 sticks)
1 cup granulated sugar
1 cup dark corn syrup
1/2 pint sour cream

Blend well, and add
1 tsp. allspice
2 T. cinnamon
1 T. ginger
1 T. cloves
1 tsp. baking soda
4-5 cups of flour

Roll out portions of the chilled dough on a well-floured board. Transfer to an ungreased cookie sheet and roll dough with a floured rolling pin to 1/8" thickness on the cookie sheet. Cut with cookie cutters or cut around your own cardboard patterns with the point of a sharp knife.
Bake at 325° for 10-15 minutes, or until browned. Cool on the pans before removing.
Decorate with white decorative icing using a decorating tube. Use regular sewing thread and a fine needle to hang the cookies.

—*Sonia Cole*

> ☆ ***Tips***
>
> *As romantic as they sound, family outings to find a Christmas tree have the potential of turning into a tortured experience in failed group decision-making. Whether searching for your tree at a Christmas tree sale in the city or venturing out to a tree farm, remember this is not a ride into the snowy woods on a one-horse open sleigh. Discuss in advance how the group will choose a tree (lessons in compromise) and caution the kids (and adults) that the perfect tree WILL NOT BE FOUND. Some families have actually come home with a tree for each family member out of sheer desperation (and fear of frostbite). Dress warmly and bring plenty of snacks.*
>
> *Good luck!*

Special Farms

Farmer Dan's

26634 SE 196th, Hobart; 15 minutes from Issaquah
432-1705
Seasonal tours offered throughout year; call for reservations
Tour prices vary

Move over Old McDonald! Farmer Dan has a farm, too, with all the animals and none of this E-I-E-I-O nonsense! The farm specializes in educational hands-on field trips for children preschool through sixth grade in groups of 12 or more. School and community groups, scouting troops and birthday parties are welcome; a minimum of 12 children is required. Guided tours feature a romp in the hay barn, a visit to the donkeys, sheep, pigs, rabbits, goats, chickens and other

animals, and lots of interesting information about farm living.

During the spring and summer tours, children help Farmer Dan plant the pumpkin patch and build the scarecrows that guard the fields until the fall harvest. In addition to pumpkins of all shapes and sizes, Farmer Dan harvests Indian corn, gourds, corn stalks and popcorn, and offers a u-cut Christmas tree farm during December; the farm is also open to the public on weekends during these special events in October and December. Group tours are offered in the spring, summer and fall by reservation.

Carnation Farm

28901 NE Carnation Farm Rd, Carnation
788-1511
Open to the public, May through October; 10 am-3 pm
Free admission
Call well in advance for group reservations; individuals may drop-in

Milk, ice cream, cheese—just ask a young child and she'll tell you they come from QFC or Safeway! Never mind the hard-working cows that make it all possible. To help explain this amazing process, Carnation Farm in the scenic Snoqualmie Valley offers an excellent opportunity to see how it all begins. This 900-acre working dairy farm is open for group and individual tours from May through October, and includes a nice self-guided walk along spotless paved pathways. The walk is suitable for strollers and wheelchairs, although it is a bit hilly. All visitors are required to register in the office, where they will be given an informative guidebook that explains each "station" of the tour.

Carnation's museum showcases a brief look at the past and present, featuring pictures of the farm's history as well as the current products of the Carnation Company. The maternity barn and calf nursery are great stops for kids, who love to pet the young calves. A visit to the milking barn will prove once and for all where the creamy white liquid originates. Additional attractions at the farm include beautiful gardens of roses, fuchsias and begonias, as well as lots of wide open grassy areas for letting off steam. The tour can be easily completed in about an hour, making it a perfect field trip for preschool and kindergarten classes, although all ages would enjoy Carnation Farm.

Remlinger Farms

32610 NE 32nd, Carnation
451-8740
Open mid-March to mid-December
Admission is free; costs for classes and activities vary

Remlinger Farms, boasting a 270-acre "working farm that really works," offers a wide variety of special events and activities for the entire family. Harvest strawberries in June, raspberries in July, pumpkins in October and Christmas trees in December, or pick up fresh vegetables and fruits, homemade jams and soups from the General Store. During the summer months, a variety of classes are offered for children including healthy cooking and eating, how the farm works, wildlife on the farm and more. Other attractions include farm tours, birthday parties and a petting farm complete with a host of farm animals, as well as special events and festivals on weekends throughout the year.

Children's Garden

4649 Sunnyside Ave N, Seattle
633-0451
Season runs during spring, summer & fall
Prices for classes vary

The Seattle Tilth Association's Children's Garden offers a series of Peawee Patch Workshops for children ages 7-12 years at its garden in Meridian Park in Wallingford. Children plant and tend their own plot in the garden, draw, keep journals, sing, play games and more. Workshops are offered June through October; call to register.

The Herbfarm

32804 Issaquah-Fall City Rd, Fall City
784-2222
Open daily year-round 10 am-5 pm; extended hours April-September
Free admission

This is a pleasant outing if your group feels like a drive into the country and a walk among lovely herb gardens. At the Herbfarm in Fall City, your family will learn more about herbs than you ever thought possible (more than most kids ever *wanted* to know)—from cultivation to cooking. The outdoor gardens feature rows and rows of an amazing variety of herbs to purchase for your home garden. The Country Store offers unusual gift ideas, as well as cookbooks and other resources for information about using herbs for medicinal, culinary and craft purposes.

Unless your children prefer watching "The Galloping Gourmet" to "Barney," it is unlikely that the majesty of these gardens will hold their attention for long. But there are llamas to look at and, on occasion, ride (call for specific information). The Herbfarm also offers picnic areas on the grounds, so bring a lunch and enjoy the rural surroundings. An exquisite lunch is served at the restaurant on the grounds, but it is far too refined and slow (and expensive) for kids. Plus, reservations must be made months in advance.

Special events are offered throughout the year, including a Halloween Adventure in October. (See the Pumpkin Harvests for more information.) Each spring, the Herbfarm offers *A Child's Garden* classes for children ages 8-12, designed to introduce kids to the joys of gardening. These classes include basic ecological concepts, how to pick a garden site, how to plant seeds, how to tell good bugs from bad, and more.

Illustration credit: The Herbfarm

Seattle P-Patch Community Gardening Program

City of Seattle, Department of Housing & Human Services

684-0264

If the preceding information has you wishing you and your kids had a garden of your own to plant and harvest—but you just don't have the space—investigate the possibilities of participating in a community P-Patch Program.

The Department of Housing & Human Services, in conjunction with the non-profit P-Patch Advisory Program, presents an opportunity for Seattle residents to organically grow any vegetable, small fruit or flower in one of the 30 garden plots located in Seattle neighborhoods. The P-Patch Program also serves refugees, low-income, disabled (some gardens are wheelchair accessible) and youth gardeners. Surplus produce is given to local food banks—the program donates 8-10 tons of fresh produce each year. The P-Patch plots range in size from 100-400 square feet, for an annual fee of $17-$48. The only requirements to participate in the program are that the gardeners be Seattle residents, contribute eight hours per year of volunteer time, attend a group work party and provide their own seeds. Call early so you'll be ready for spring planting.

Farmers Markets

If there is just no time to get out of town or the weather is too wet to send you off into your own yard (imagine!), take the kids to one of the area's many farmers markets. Rich in colors, sights, smells and sounds, these markets present a plentiful array of fresh-from-the-garden vegetables, fruits and flowers, clothes and jewelry from local craftman and street artists that will fully captivate your child.

Issaquah Farmer's Market
105 Newport Way SW, Issaquah
Open April-October
Saturday, 9 am-3 pm

Kent Saturday Market
Corner of Second & Smith streets, downtown Kent
Open May-October
Saturday, 9 am-4 pm

Pike Place Market
First Avenue & Pike Street, downtown Seattle
Open year-round
Monday-Saturday, 10 am-6 pm; Sunday, 11 am-5 pm; Sunday is an optional day for vendors; not all stores may choose to open
See In & Around Downtown/Pike Place Market for details.

Redmond Saturday Market
7730 Leary Way, Redmond
Open May-October
Saturday, 8 am-2 pm

University District
University Heights Community Center, University Way and 50th NE
Open June-October
Saturday, 9 am-1 pm

Vashon Saturday Market
Located in downtown Vashon on the Vashon Highway
Open year-round; major season runs April-December
Saturday, 10 am-3 pm

Winslow Saturday Market
Located within walking distance of ferry dock
Open May-September
Saturday, 9 am-2 pm

CHAPTER 3

Parks

If you think your neighborhood park is the best in the area, you are not alone. Families all over Puget Sound feel the same way about *their* neighborhood parks, which can mean only one thing: we have an abundance of top-notch parks. And we're not just talking about places with good swing sets and playgrounds.

Does your park have a great kiddie beach? A Japanese garden? Nature and wildlife trails? A good kite-flying area? Giant wind chimes? Someone's neighborhood does. So next time your children want to go to the park, make it a new adventure instead of a routine skip down the block.

Most of the parks departments publish excellent guides that feature listings of parks and other recreation areas, location maps, and details about various facilities. To obtain these publications call: King County, 296-4232; Seattle 684-4075; Bellevue, 455-6881; Issaquah, 392-1008; Kirkland, 828-1217; Mercer Island, 236-3545; and Redmond, 556-2300.

All of the parks in the region offer good picnic spots, but if you are planning a get-together with a large group and want to be sure you'll have enough tables when you show up, sheltered sites may be reserved year-round. Picnic sites in Seattle may be reserved at Alki, Carkeek, Discovery, Gas Works, Golden Gardens, Lincoln, Seward, and Woodland. Cost varies from $12 to $54. Reservations are taken beginning in March each year; call early for best sites (684-4081).

Alki Beach

Alki Ave SW, Seattle

When the first Seattle settlers landed on Alki, they were optimistic that eventually the area would become a bustling town. The name they gave their settlement was New York Alki (Alki meaning "by and by" in Chinook jargon). No matter what those pioneers envisioned, one can be sure it *wasn't* the California beach scene that characterizes this two-and-a-half mile strip during the summer months. Hordes of skaters, cyclists and folks just checking each other out descend upon this stretch of Alki Ave on hot summer days. (The high volume of teen car traffic has been curtailed with a recent city council ban on "cruising.") However, the crush of humanity that flocks to the shore when the sun is out is not around most of the year. Year-round the beach offers families fine beachcombing, a fresh sea breeze and an expansive view of the city skyline and the Olympic Mountains. Take along hot dogs and marshmallows if the weather is decent (small beach fires allowed) and bring a kite to fly upon the sea breezes.

☆ *Tips*

The Coast Guard Auxiliary offers free tours of the Alki Point Light Station on weekends and on some holidays from noon to 4 pm. No reservations are necessary. They also will give group tours on Wednesdays by prior reservation. To arrange a special Wednesday tour, call 286-5423 weekdays.

There is a good bike trail that runs from Alki to Lincoln Park (Active Play: Outdoor Fun).

☆ *Essentials*

Alki is a fun place to head for a change-of-pace lunch or dinner. Across the street from the beach are numerous "boardwalk" eateries.

For some of the best fish and chips in the area, or for that matter, the city, check out Spud Fish and Chips (2666 Alki Ave SW, 938-0606). Spuds is best known for their good-sized chucks of fresh ling cod coated in cornmeal and fried in canola oil. If the kids don't like fish or clams or oysters, they can carbo-load on the delicious fries (peeled, cut and fried fresh every day). Spuds is also located near Green Lake at 6860 Green Lake Way N, 524-0565; and in Kirkland at 9700 NE Juanita Dr, 823-0607. (Open lunch and dinner everyday.)

Pegasus Pizza (2758 Alki Ave SW, 932-4849) serves up fabulous pizza (try the Greek pizza) in an attractive setting with plenty of windows to enjoy the fine views. Dine inside and enjoy the friendly staff or use the take-out window and picnic on the beach. (Open everyday dinner only.)

Bellevue Downtown Park

At the south end of Bellevue Square, Bellevue

This island of green space, completed in 1990, is a welcome addition to downtown Bellevue. Large grassy areas, beautiful gardens, fountains, a cascading 240-foot-wide waterfall, a 1200-foot canal and a special play area—complete with climbing toys and swings—give parents and kids a place to unwind after a shopping spree in nearby Bellevue Square. The park is a great place to fly a kite and a popular spot for public concerts and special activities during the spring and summer months.

☆ *Essentials*

McDonald's, Arby's, Jack-in-the-Box and Kentucky Fried Chicken are all close to Bellevue Downtown Park, so if you are hankering for a picnic on a nice day, but you don't feel like packing a lunch, you have several convenient options.

Bellefield Nature Park

1905 188th SE, Bellevue

To get there: Take I-405 from either I-90 or SR 520; exit at SE 8th and head west on SE 8th. Turn left on 118th SE. Drive one-half mile to the parking area. The trail begins 50 feet further south on the road.

When the Montlake Ship Canal was completed in 1916, the level of Lake Washington went down by nine feet. The 48 acres that now form Bellefield Nature Park (sometimes called Bellevue Nature Park) were transformed from a shallow backwater of Lake Washington to an area of marsh and deciduous trees. Later, to develop blueberry farming, the land was further drained. Overlake Farm, the largest blueberry farm in the region, still operates across from the slough.

There used to be numerous trails criss-crossing the interior of the park, but in the interest of preserving the marsh, only the perimeter trail—a one-mile loop—remains. The path is well-maintained, thanks to the efforts of volunteers from the Seattle Audubon Society; the Audubon adopted the park in recognition of its value as a wildlife habitat.

In the park you'll find Mercer Slough, which connects Lake Washington to Kelsey Creek. You and your kids may spot a wide variety of water fowl and marsh birds among the cattails, including great blue herons and kingfishers, as well as frogs, garter snakes, tadpoles and toads. Wear boots or old shoes and stay on the path—the bog is deceptively deep in some places.

Camp Long

5200 35th SW, Seattle
684-7434
Lodge hours: Tues-Sun, 8:30 am-5 pm, except holidays

With 68 acres of forest, nature trails, a 25-foot artificial climbing rock (Schurman Rock) and plenty of open areas, Camp Long is the ideal park to visit when the family wants to get away from it all without driving far.

For many years, Seattle Parks & Recreation operated Camp Long exclusively for organized groups, who could reserve the lodge or outlying cabins for day or overnight use. Today, the special programs offered to groups continue, but this gem of a park and the outstanding nature classes are open to the public as well.

At the beautiful old lodge next to the parking lot, you'll find an interesting historical and wildlife exhibit and an informative park ranger, who will give you the run-down on how to enjoy the park.

The Animal Tracks Nature Trail is a half-mile loop through the woods, which is perfect for young hikers who are long on enthusiasm but short on endurance. An excellent interpretive booklet, which is keyed to the numbered posts along this trail, can be purchased at the lodge for $3. It contains fascinating information about the plants and animals that inhabit these woods. To get to the trail, follow the path down the hill from the lodge to the open field below. Take a left on the service road, passing Polliwog Pond on the right. At the north end of the pond, leave the road as it curves right and instead follow the path past the large, flat stone compass set in the ground to the sign marking the start of the trail. Start on the left fork.

Don't leave the park without visiting the "Glacier"—a rock structure built into the wooded hill just north of Schurman Rock. It is used to train climbers in rappelling, but kids love the challenge of scrambling to the top of the slope (closely supervised by an adult).

An enormous open field sits in the middle of Camp Long—ideal for games that require plenty of space. A pond sits north of the field and there's a large campfire pit surrounded by benches at the south end of the park. Free nature walks, led by camp naturalists, are offered every Saturday from 2-3:30 pm. These are fine outings for all ages (adults need to accompany children, no registration required). You and your kids will come away enriched, knowing more about the flora and fauna that thrive in Northwest forests as well as the Native Americans who also thrived in these woods for many years.

☆ *Tips*

Excellent, very reasonably priced programs are offered throughout the year for children (as well as adults) at Camp Long, including wildlife workshops, campouts and, once a month, a climbing class on Schurman Rock for ages seven and up.

For a back-to-nature overnight, not too far from latte land, rent a rustic cabin in the park, complete with bunk beds and electricity for $15/night. Bring your friends—the cabins each have six double bunks and sleep twelve. If you need a wheel-chair accessible cabin, there are three. The wheelchair-friendly Rolling Hills Trail starts at the parking lot and provides access to these cabins. Call 684-7434 for cabin rental and class information.

"Whispering of the Woods" is an outstanding teacher's guide full of interesting facts and suggested activities to make a trip to Camp Long more meaningful. Available for $8 at the lodge.

Children's Park

Island Crest Way, Mercer Island

This is a pleasant little park designed by the Mercer Island Preschool Association especially for small children. The play equipment is imaginative and fun. Two tennis courts are nearby, and several short trails meander through the shady grounds.

Coulon Park

1201 Lake Washington Blvd N, Renton

Located at the southern-most shore of Lake Washington, next to Boeing's Renton plant, Coulon Park is the city's pride and a youngster's dream. The major attraction, aside from the award-winning architecture of the pavilion and restaurant, is the large sandy swimming beach. The kids will quickly target the play area, which sits adjacent to the beach and is fully equipped with slides, swings, climbing toys and a big sandbox. They'll also enjoy crossing a foot bridge to a small island that features a climbing tower and fort. Other attractions include shuffleboard, horseshoe pits and volleyball and tennis courts. Boat rentals were available until recently; the budget will dictate whether they'll be offered again.

☆ *Essentials*

At the northern side of Coulon Park is an Ivar's Fish Bar, where you can sit outside and enjoy your lunch while watching the action on the water. If you'd rather take your own picnic, the large, covered pavilion has outstanding picnic facilities,

Photo credit: Paul Dowling

At Discovery Park there are beaches, forests and meadows to explore.

including several barbecue grills.

If there is one drawback to the park, it's the abundance of geese: Be prepared with washable blankets or towels to sit on!

There is plenty of parking, even on the sunniest days.

Discovery Park

3801 W Government Way, Seattle
386-4236

When the Secretary of the Army announced in 1964 that 85% of the land at Fort Lawton in Magnolia would become surplus, local and federal politicians went to work on obtaining the land for public enjoyment. In 1972, the feds bequeathed the City of Seattle with a 391-acre site, which was aptly named Discovery (after Puget Sound explorer Captain George Vancouver's flagship, the H.M.S. Discovery). The park opened in 1973 and was awarded more land in 1975. Today the military buildings and trucks that remain are the only reminders of this park's military past.

Discovery Park is now the largest and most diverse park in Seattle, boasting 534 acres of forest, meadows, cliffs, beaches, self-guided interpretive loops, short trails, jogging trails, man-made ponds and a thriving population of birds and animals. It's a spectacular nature sanctuary that invites exploration and learning, as well as sport and play.

The south meadow, once maintained as an athletic field for military personnel, is today an inviting open space with a majestic view of Puget Sound and the Olympics. It is a fine spot to spread a blanket and delve into a good book, while the kids romp or fly a kite (there is always a stiff breeze off the Sound). The South Bluff, further east of the meadow, offers a spectacular vista of the mountains and islands beyond, but the cliffs are steep and treacherous, so be careful to hold on tightly to your curious preschooler. One of the most popular attractions at this bluff is a big pile of sand (fondly referred to by locals as "the dunes," despite its singularity), upon which such games as King of the Mountain and Bury the Feet can be played. At the higher point of the South Bluff, you will see signs that lead you down to the South Beach and the West Point area, renowned for some of the best marine bird watching and tidepooling in Seattle. The beach, like the park, is mixed terrain: there are sandy areas, rocky beds and mudflats (when the tide is low).

The North Bluff was once the site of military barracks and the non-commissioned officer's club. Here, you'll find another spectacular view and several picnic tables. On the area of land below the bluff, the Shilhoh people lived until early in this century. To the left of the picnic area is a trail leading down to the North Beach—another ideal spot for exploring tidepools. Look for crabs, sea stars, sea anemones and sea urchins. Remember to tell the kids to look but leave the sealife undisturbed—lucky for the animals, the days of hauling sea creatures home in buckets have passed.

The trails that penetrate the park each offer a different view of Discovery. For exercise buffs, there's a fitness trail (with workout stations); the Loop Trail is a 2.8-mile loop full of curves and twists through wood and meadow. A great walk for families is the Wolf Tree Nature Trail—a lovely half-mile path through one of the least disturbed areas (last logged in the 1860s). Numbered posts designate points of interest, which can be interpreted by an excellent booklet, available for purchase (35 cents) or for free (if you return it) at the Visitor's Center (located inside the east gate, to the left). To get to the trail from the main east gate entrance, follow the park road to the north parking lot. At the southwest corner of the lot is an information sign with a map of the park. Wolf Tree Trail begins at the northwest corner of the lot, next to the gated road leading to the Daybreak Star Center.

There are also free drop-in nature walks led by knowledgeable and contagiously enthusiastic park rangers every Saturday at 2 pm. Meet at the Visitor's Center.

One highlight of Discovery Park that is not nature-made is Daybreak Star Center, a Native American cultural/educational center in the northwest corner of the park. Twelve Native American artists were commissioned to create artworks for this beautiful building,

☆ ***Tips***

Discovery Park rangers offer an exceptional opportunity to learn about the natural environment of our region with a variety of programs for adults and kids. The popular Night Walks, on which rangers lead families on a search for the nocturnal life of the park, are just one example of the many activities offered. The classes and workshops are low-cost (or free) and invariably top-notch. Call 386-4236 for information.

There are several bald eagles living at the park—ask the rangers at the Visitor's Center where you can spot their nests. Bring binoculars!

and most of the pieces are large murals and carvings depicting legends and traditions that children will find interesting. Daybreak Star's gallery and gift shop feature a variety of contemporary and traditional Native American art, including beadwork, baskets and a large assortment of Native American dolls.

On the second Saturday of each month, from October through April, an Indian Art Mart is held from 11 am to 4 pm at Daybreak Star. It usually includes an authentic Native American lunch of salmon, corn and Indian-fry bread. Lunch costs $7/person.

There is no charge to visit Daybreak Star Center. If you park in the north parking lot at Discovery Park, it is a short walk to the center. Check the map in the southwestern corner of the north lot for directions. Hours: Mon-Sat, 10 am-5 pm; Sun 12-5 pm. Phone: 285-4425.

☆ ***Essentials***

The park can be entered at the main gate at W Government Way and 36th, the south gate at W Emerson near Magnolia Blvd W and the north gate near W Commodore Way and 40th W. Unless you know where you are going, it is easiest to enter at the main gate on the east side, where you'll find a good map and a short history of the park and the Visitor's Center just ahead on the left.

Just south of the Visitor's Center, you'll find tennis courts, a basketball court and an exceptionally good playground (none of which is visible from the parking lot). Picnic tables can be found at a number of locations: along the North Bluff, near the playground (south of the Visitor's Center), at West Point and at the Daybreak Arts Center.

The location of restrooms is a good thing to scope out when taking little kids to this big park. You'll find them at the Visitor's Center, South Meadow, North Bluff and West Point.

Farrel-McWhirter Park

19545 Redmond Rd, Redmond

This 68-acre park on the edge of Redmond consists of a lush second-growth forest, encompassing a large open field, an orchard and a children's farm. Two miles of trails wind through the forest. Charlotte's Trail, an asphalt trail that is wheelchair accessible, runs the length of the park. The Mackey Creek Watershed Trail is a self-guided, interpretive half-mile loop. There is also a one-and-a-half mile equestrian loop.

In the 1930s, the McWhirter family built the farm on this land for a summer home. Elise Farrel-McWhirter, a horse trainer, willed the property to the City of Redmond, and upon her death in 1971, the land became a public park. The setting is inviting and exciting for kids, who'll love visiting the pigs, rabbits, goats, ponies and chickens that inhabit the children's farm. Even the restroom, located in a converted silo, is worthy of exploration—it has a fun lookout on top. The Redmond Parks Department hosts a variety of excellent programs for children of all ages at Farrel-McWhirter, including farm activities, preschool classes, breakfasts with the animals, pony rides and summer day camps. Call 556-2300 for program information.

Gas Works Park

Northlake Way at Meridian, Seattle

When park designers first presented the idea of leaving the old gas works plant perched at the north end of Lake Union as an integral part of a new park, there were noisy critics galore. Today, the grotesque remnants have become a familiar part of the cityscape, and the park a premier spot to enjoy a picnic and an unobstructed view of the downtown skyline.

A working gas refinery until 1955, about one-third of the old machinery still stands in Gas Works Park. The old boiler house with an overhead maze of pipes has become a brightly painted play barn, and its neighbor, a grassy manmade knoll, has become a favorite gathering spot for kite-flying enthusiasts.

Look for a giant sundial, built in the ground near the top of the grassy hill. Made of inlaid and cast bronze, shells, ceramic and found objects that have been embedded in multicolored concrete, the dial measures 28 feet in diameter. To tell time, the viewer stands on a central oval and becomes the gnomon for the sundial, casting a shadow toward the mosaic hour markers at the perimeter. Children will delight in closely examining the dial to discover small figures, sea life and other objects set in this beautiful piece of public art.

> ☆ ***Tips***
>
> *Gas Works Park marks the west end of the Burke Gilman Trail and is a good place to take a restroom stop and stretch your legs. It's also a very popular picnic spot on a summer night; call 684-4081 to reserve tables for a large group.*

Photo credit: Paul Dowling

Beachcombing at Golden Gardens.

Golden Gardens

North end of Seaview NW, Seattle

If you hanker for a beach fire and salt air, head to Golden Gardens on Shilshole Bay, at the west end of Ballard. The water is frigid, but there is a warmer stream running into the Sound that is just right for water play. Ice cream and fish and chips are within easy walking distance. No lifeguards on duty.

Grass Lawn Park

NE 70th St & 148th Ave NE, Bellevue

Located where Redmond, Bellevue and Kirkland intersect, Grass Lawn Park offers plenty of space and activities for all ages. A play area, featuring climbing apparatus and swings, is set in a woodsy, nicely shaded spot. Children, preschool-age and older, will enjoy riding their bikes and trikes along the paved pathways. Also features baseball and soccer fields and tennis courts.

☆ ***Tips***

In response to a rowdy teen scene that was spoiling the peace for the surrounding neighborhood, city police now close Golden Gardens at dusk—so forget any thoughts of a weenie roast under the stars. Be prepared to have your sunset enjoyment cut short by the blast of bullhorns telling you to vacate the area.

For a fabulous beach walk, head out to Golden Gardens at a minus tide and walk north along a wide expanse of sand and rocks. If you walk far enough, you might run across geoduck diggers uncovering those grotesque mollusks. From out on the sand, you're likely to see a few trains pass by on the tracks above the beach—always a good diversion for young kids.

Green Lake

E Green Lake Dr N & W Green Lake Dr N, Seattle

Many Seattleites exercise religiously, and Green Lake has long been their Mecca. Joggers, roller skaters, cyclists and boaters—of all shapes, sizes and abilities—make their homage to the lake whenever weather permits (and often when it doesn't). Families, too, flock to Green Lake, because it offers plentiful picnic areas, as well as activities for all ages. There's a fabulous playground (at the east entrance), lifeguarded beaches from mid-June through Labor Day, a big wading pool (northeast corner), a community center, boat rentals, an indoor swimming pool and many nearby places to grab a tasty snack or meal. The paved jogging/bicycle trail, which runs along the water's edge (about 2.8 miles), is very popular on sunny weekends and gets dangerously crowded for wobbly young walkers, skaters and bikers.

☆ ***Essentials***

Dining opportunities are abundant near the lake. For starters, you can grab a regular-joe ice cream cone at Baskin-Robbins 31 Ice Cream at the southeast corner of the lake (near Gregg's Greenlake Cycle), or a gourmet (more expensive) frozen treat at Haagen-Dazs, which sits at the south side (west of Albertson's). Next to Haagen-Dazs, tasty grilled hot dogs are served up at The Frankfurter. Try a kosher beef frank, fresh squeezed lemonade and a chocolate chip cookie. Spuds Fish and Chips, also located on the southside of the lake, serves up some of the finest fish and chips in town. Just one block off the lake, you'll find one of the more popular of the 12 locations of Toshi's Teriyaki (1406 N 80th St, take-out only). Four bucks will buy you a hefty serving of lip-smacking good beef or chicken teriyaki, a generous scoop of steamed rice and a tangy cabbage salad. Kids typically love the sweet/salty teriyaki flavor as much as their parents, and one order is generous enough to split between two youngsters.

☆ ***Tips***

Across the street from the northeast end of Green Lake, you'll find one of the finest children's bookstores in the region, the Secret Garden Children's Bookshop (7900 E Green Lake Dr N, 524-4556). Take a break from the sun and browse with the kids.

Duck feeding, which used to be big fun for little ones at Green Lake, is now prohibited because a surge in the duck and geese populations has created a nuisance and health hazard.

The popularity of Green Lake threatens to ruin the pleasure—especially when families extra-burdened by hauling kids and their assorted paraphernalia have difficulty finding a place to park on a hot day. It is best enjoyed with little kids when the weather is less than spectacular and the crowd has dwindled. See Biking, Boating and Skating in Active Play: Outdoor Fun; see Swimming Pools and Indoor Playgrounds for Toddlers and Preschoolers in the Active Play: Indoor Fun chapter for more information about activities at Green Lake.

At the northside of the lake, round the corner from the Secret Garden bookstore, Ed's Juice and Java serves up a mean fresh fruit juice or latte, and across the street, the Urban Bakery offers delicious sandwiches, baked goods, salads, etc. On the other side of the Secret Garden, Guido's serves up fabulous pizza and there's also a new frozen yogurt spot called Bumpy's where you pick the flavor, and they make sumptuous frozen yogurt right before your eyes—kids will delight in watching the process almost as much as eating the final product.

Hiram M. Chittenden Government Locks

3015 NW 54th in Ballard
783-7001 (783-7059 for tour information)
Open to public viewing daily, 7 am- 9 pm
Visitor's Center is open Oct-May 11 am-5 pm, every day except Tues & Wed. Open June-Sept, every day, 10 am-7 pm
Public tours Saturdays & Sundays, Oct-May at 2 pm; June 1-30, 1 pm & 3:30 pm; July 1-Sept 30, 1 pm & 3 pm

The difference between the water level of Puget Sound and Lake Washington varies by anywhere from 6 to 26 feet. The locks protect the ecosystem of the lake by preventing salt water from entering Lake Washington when boats go from Puget Sound into Lake Washington. Most people, regardless of age, are fascinated by the remarkable sight of boats and water rising and dropping right before their eyes. On a warm afternoon bring a a picnic to enjoy on the grassy knoll above the locks and watch the boat traffic parade past. (Sundays are great for boat watching because many people are returning from their weekends in the San Juans).

There are also fish ladders next to the locks with underwater viewing of the salmon as they struggle to return to their spawning grounds. Salmon spawning is from April through September.

The Visitor's Center offers slide shows and a working model that explains the mechanics of the locks, and staff are available to answer questions. Tours begin in the Visitor's Center, then proceed to the gardens, the locks and the fish ladders (see above for tour hours).

The locks have gained a reputation among sea lions as a five-star fish restaurant. One sea lion became such a frequent patron he was named "Herschel" by the local media, who enjoyed reporting on his skill and persistance in outwitting every imaginable effort to gently but firmly stop him from dining on the salmon. (They even shipped him down to California but he swam right back up the coast.) So look closely and you may spot a persistent sea lion enjoying a meal.

Kelsey Creek Community Park/Farm

13204 SE 8th Pl, Bellevue
See Animals, Animals, Animals

Kubota Gardens

55th Ave S & Renton Ave S, Seattle

This 20-acre display garden is the most recent addition to the Seattle Parks system. Waterfalls, exquisite gardens, prayer stones and lush lawns offer an oasis of calm and a fitting tribute to Fijitaro Kubota and his descendants, who cultivated these gardens and worked to promote American understanding of Japanese culture. Steep trails wind to the high point of the property, which offers a view of the gardens, the Cascade mountain range and the Eastside. The gardens are open to the public every day during daylight hours free of charge.

Lake Sammamish State Park

20606 SE 56th St, Issaquah
455-7010

A large, sandy swimming beach is the main draw to this huge park that sits at the south end of Lake Sammamish. Complete with swings, climbing equipment, food concessions and plenty of room for volleyball (bring your own net), the park is very popular for family reunions, as well as company and school picnics. Reserve your picnic tables if you are bringing a big group by calling 455-7010. If you have any fishing enthusiasts in the group, tell them to bring along their poles for Issaquah Creek, which runs directly through the park. If you tire of the beach, Gilman Village on the south side of I-90 offers good browsing and numerous snack opportunities.

☆ ***Tips***

Though Colman Pool started as a tide-fed swimming pool, it has steadily been improved to become the first-class, Olympic-sized, outdoor, heated saltwater pool that it is today. Situated right at the edge of the beach at Lincoln Park, Colman is maintained by the Seattle Department of Parks & Recreation and is open summers only. Call 684-7494 for more information.

The short, easy trek from Lincoln Park's parking lot, through deep woods, down to the saltwater beach is likely to seem much longer and much steeper to the little ones when it's time to go home after a frolic on the beach. Be prepared to bribe and coax your short-legged hiking companions up the hill, or bring a carrier to tote them on your back.

The Alki bike path connects Lincoln Park with Alki Beach. See Active Play: Outdoor Fun for more details.

Lincoln Park

Fauntleroy SW & SW Webster, West Seattle

Spread on 130 acres at one of the most scenic vantage points in the region, Lincoln Park offers breathtaking views of the Olympics and Puget Sound, as well as woods, ample wide-open playing fields, a fine stretch of beach (less crowded than nearby Alki) and the recently renovated outdoor swimming pool, Colman Pool. A short hike down a forest bluff takes you to the beach, where there is plenty of sand and a pleasant cement boardwalk. The park is located right next to the Vashon-Southworth Ferry dock; kids will enjoy watching the ferries come and go.

Luther Burbank Park

2040 84th Ave SE, Mercer Island
296-4438

This park, which covers 77 acres on the eastern shore of Mercer Island, is a local favorite among families. The clean, sandy beach, with its shallow swimming areas and ideal sandcastle spots, is a paradise for young children. And if that's not enough to keep the kiddos occupied, a wooded trail along the water's edge will take them to a top-notch playground full of slides, tunnels, swings, balance beams, crawling nets and the like.

Photo credit: Paul Dowling

Luther Burbank Park on Mercer Island is a great place to build sandcastles.

☆ *Essentials*

Luther Burbank's north parking lot provides access to the playground; go to the south parking lot if you are headed for the beach. Try not to pack too much, as it's still a good walk from the parking lot to the beach. If you plan to bring food, keep in mind that the picnic area by the beach (which has barbecue grills) gets crowded on summer weekends. Call ahead for reservations if you are bringing a big group.

Magnuson Park

Sand Point Way NE & 65th NE, Seattle

This 193-acre park lies on the western shores of Lake Washington, next to what remains of the Sand Point Naval Air Base. Due to its relatively recent conversion from a military air base to a park, it is a rather desolate strip of land, barren of the lush woods that characterize the other large city parks. Nonetheless, the paths along the shore are ideal for walkers as well as novice cyclists and skaters. Other features include a good swimming beach (with lifeguards), abundant picnic tables, softball and soccer fields, and

☆ ***Tips***

At the north end of Magnuson Park lies one of the most charming outdoor art sites in the city. Passage through a gate at the end of the park walkway marks the end of the city park land and the start of NOAA (National Oceanographic and Atmospheric Administration) property. NOAA developed its 114-acre site by integrating the shoreline walk with artworks that emphasize the relationship between man and nature. The result is a wonderful place to experience the outdoors and art with your kids.

A short distance past the gate separating the NOAA site from the park, walkers cross a footbridge lined with passages from Melville's Moby Dick. *Just to the left of the bridge, a short path leads to the Sound Garden, a sculpture of steel towers holding aluminum pipes that wail eerily when the wind blows. Listeners have to be very still and quiet to hear the soft and haunting sounds emanating from the sculpture, so convince the kids to sit down on one of the benches and take advantage of a few calm moments. The NOAA site opens every day at 6:30 am.*

six tennis courts. With its long shore and open layout, the park rarely feels crowded.

Marymoor Park

6064 W Lake Sammamish Pkwy NE, Redmond

Covering 520 acres, Marymoor is the second largest park in the King County park system. In addition to the numerous athletic fields that make the park a popular center for soccer and softball games, Marymoor also features a velodrome for bicyclists, climbing equipment and swings, miles of walking and bicycle trails, and lots of wide-open spaces perfect for kite flying and remote-controlled airplanes. The Sammamish River Trail runs right through the park, and a three-mile walk or bike ride will take you from Marymoor to the wineries in Woodinville (see Biking in the Active Play: Outdoor Fun chapter). Also, folks who want to spend some lazy hours drifting upon the Sammamish Slough in inner tubes or rafts often start at Marymoor. For obvious reasons, the park is usually jammed on hot summer days.

With all the action at Marymoor, it is easy to overlook the Marymoor Interpretive Trail, a short (just under a mile) path to the Lake Sammamish overlook, featuring informative signs about the plants, animals and birds that thrive in this wildlife preserve (no dogs allowed). The walk can be lengthened by taking the boardwalk north along the Sammamish River, walking over open fields to the parking lots for a loop almost two miles long.

As you walk along the trail, try to impress your kids by telling them that from 1964 to 1970 archaeologists from the University of Washington identified four pre-Columbian sites, two in Marymoor Park and two more just outside the park along the river. The oldest tools found were made 6,000 years ago, the rest around 3,000 years ago. The artifacts can be seen at the Burke Museum on the UW campus (see Kid Culture/Exhibits & Museums).

The more recent history of Marymoor can be discovered in the park itself. James Clise, a Seattle banker, purchased this land in 1904 for use as a bird-hunting reserve. The 28-room lodge that he built is called the Clise Mansion and houses the Marymoor Museum (885-3684). Museum exhibits highlight the history of the Eastside and the park. Admission is free; hours are Tues, Wed and Thurs, 11 am-4 pm; Sun 1-4 pm.

☆ Tips

See the Spectator Sports chapter for details about bike races at the Velodrome.

The Heritage Festival is a fun event for families that occurs every July in Marymoor. Go early and expect heavy traffic getting into the park.

Matthew's Beach

NE 93rd & Sand Point Way NE, Seattle

Matthew's Beach is a popular park with families during the summer. The lifeguarded beach is an exceptionally good swimming area, easily accessible from the parking lot—a real plus for parents who are packing the usual assortment of beach and kid equipment. Located in close proximity to the Burke Gilman Trail, Matthew's is also a good place to get off the bikes and enjoy a quick swim and picnic. A snazzy new playground adds to the fun.

Meydenbauer Park

419 98th Ave NE, Bellevue

Located on the shores of Meydenbauer Bay in Bellevue, this park is nestled—almost hidden—among tall trees and residential areas. The grounds were recently refurbished, and swings and climbing equipment were set right on the sandy beach. There are plenty of shady picnic areas, but try to pack light, as the walk from the car is a long one if you're loaded down with gear.

Myrtle Edwards Park

Alaskan Way between W Bay & W Thomas, Seattle

Located just north of Pier 70 on the Seattle waterfront, Myrtle Edwards is a scenic strip along Elliott Bay, which has two paved paths: one for walking and one for cycling (see Biking in Active Play: Outdoor Fun). The grassy areas are limited, the benches abundant, but don't think that's all the park has to offer. In its short stretch you will discover a grain terminal (that huge white monstrosity); a fishing pier (Pier 86), replete with a bait and tackle shop (see Fishing in Active Play: Outdoor Fun); a sand pit between the two trails about midway down the strip; and a gigantic rock sculpture, *Adjacent, Against, Upon,* to climb and explore (near the south entrance). Moreover, you'll discover a cool sea breeze and a panoramic view.

☆ *Essentials*

Myrtle Edwards is a good place to take a stroll at sunset, after a big meal at the Old Spaghetti Factory (see Basics/Restaurants).

If you want to get from Myrtle Edwards to Pioneer Square without dealing with parking hassles, take the Waterfront Streetcar—it leaves from Broad St, near the south entrance to the park.

Newcastle Beach

4400 Lake Washington Blvd S, Bellevue

Newcastle Beach, the newest park in the Bellevue Parks system, is located on Lake Washington between Bellevue and Renton, just south of Newport Shores Marina. The 28-acre park is wonderful for kids—flat and wide open, with a nice shallow swimming area and a sandy beach. Near the beach is a first-rate playground, with swings, slides and climbing equipment. The park, which has its own wildlife reserve, also features nature trails and a fishing dock.

St. Edward State Park

1445 Juanita Dr NE, Bothell
823-2992
To get there: Take I-90 or SR 520 east to I-405. Drive north on 405 to exit 20A (NE 116th St). Go west on 116th to 98th Ave NE in Kirkland. Cross the intersection and continue on Juanita Dr. In about four and three quarters miles, turn left on NE 145th St, where signs announce the Saint Thomas Center and Milham Recovery Center (there are no signs marking the park on this road). In two-tenths of a mile, turn right and drive straight ahead to reach the parking lot.

When the Catholic diocese closed the seminary that had occupied this 316-acre forested property since 1931, the state snapped it up. It was a wise purchase, considering that the area has 3,000 feet of waterfront—the largest remaining undeveloped shoreline on Lake Washington.

Also included in the deal, were a gymnasium, tennis courts, outdoor handball courts, baseball fields, an indoor swimming pool, soccer fields, picnic areas, and about seven miles of trails. Many of the trails lead to the beach but swimming is not advised, as there are no lifeguards and the shoreline drops away abruptly about 30 feet out. The swimming pool and the gymnasium at St. Edward Park are run by the King County Parks system. (The gymnasium is, however, closed for renovation and will re-open in the summer of 1994.) The 25-yard pool is open to the public for public swims most mornings and evenings year-round, with afternoon hours in the summertime. Cost is $1.25/ person. Lessons are available. Call 296-2970 for more details.

Saltwater State Park

25205 8th Pl S, Kent
764-4128
To get there: Take exit 149 (Hwy 516, Kent-Des Moines) west off I-5. Drive west on 516 to SR 509 (Marine View Dr) until it veers left. Continue right on 8th Pl S into the park.

Put 88 acres of forest park on the edge of Puget Sound, just outside the city, and designate it as one of the few overnight camping sites in the Seattle-Tacoma region. Add boating, hiking, scuba diving and swimming, and you get the most-used state park in the area: Saltwater State Park. Many of the overnight camp sites are next to McSourley Creek, which winds down the park's ravine; the steep, wooded hillside absorbs the noise of the nearby bridge traffic to give campers and hikers some unexpected quiet. You don't have to be a camper to enjoy this park, but you'll likely wait in line at the gate on sunny summer weekends (no fee for day use). Try going after Labor Day to avoid the crowds, and be sure to seek out the sandy swimming beach—it's one of the best on the Sound. Clamming is also good here, so pack up the buckets and shovels, and let the kids dig for dinner. (January to June only, call 800-562-5632 for a red-tide report.) See Clamming in the Active Play: Outdoor Fun chapter.

Seward Park

Lake Washington Blvd S and S Juneau St, Seattle

Situated at the end of a long scenic drive along Lake Washington Blvd, this 277-acre park covers an entire peninsula. A two-and-a-half mile loop around the outside of the park is very popular with walkers, joggers and cyclists (see Biking in Active Play: Outdoor Fun). One point of interest is the fish hatchery run by the University of Washington located on the east side of this road. There are also six picnic shelters.

Though the lower part of the park, next to the lake, jumps with action on a hot summer day, the old-growth forest above remains cool and tranquil. Several broad trails penetrate the woods in the park; the closed road that leads to the top of the park, past the playground and amphitheater, is perhaps most inviting for strolling.

☆ Tips

The Seward Park Art Studio (722-6342) offers an extensive and well regarded program of art classes for both children and adults.

Photo credit: Paul Dowling

The conservatory at Volunteer Park.

Volunteer Park

15th E & E Prospect, Seattle

This elegant old park on Capitol Hill has recently become an even better place for kids with the addition of a fine new playground on the site of the former play area near the popular wading pool. In an impressive neighborhood effort, Capitol Hill families raised money to gain matching funds from the city and helped develop the design for the playground. The result is an imaginative assortment of play equipment for a wide age range.

The former home of the Seattle Art Museum, Volunteer Park features stately lawns and gardens; a 75-foot water tower that can be climbed (daily 8:30 am-5:30 pm); a conservatory; and the *Black Sun* sculpture by Isamu Noguchi, which overlooks the reservoir and frames a spectacular view of the city and Olympic Mountains beyond. The circular, black granite sculpture is irresistible for children, who like to crawl through the slippery, big opening in its center.

Volunteer Park's conservatory, located at the north end of the park, envelopes its visitors in lush greenery, sweet heavy fragrance and humid air. This splendid glass structure houses monstrous cacti, breathtaking orchids and other flora that will capture most children's attention. The tropical warmth of the conservatory is especially welcome on a cold wintry day.

The conservatory is open to the public daily, including all holidays. Hours are 9 am-7 pm from the first of May to mid-Sept; 9 am-5 pm the rest of the year. Admission is free.

Washington Park Arboretum

Lake Washington Blvd E between E Madison & Hwy 520, Seattle

The 200-acre Arboretum is on city property, but it is managed by the Center for Urban Horticulture at the University of Washington. This isn't a typical park with bike paths and playgrounds, but rather a place where you'll discover miles of walking paths, mossy ponds and the finest display of native Northwest plants found anywhere in the region. A fun way to enjoy the Arboretum is by rowboat or canoe, available for rental from the UW Boat House (see Boating in Active Play: Outdoor Fun).

The Japanese Garden is one of the Arboretum's highlights. An authentic Japanese stroll garden, designed by Japanese landscape designer Juki Iida and maintained by the Seattle Department of Parks and Recreation, the garden offers a peaceful reprieve from city activity. Open from March through November, visitors are welcome to pick up a brochure at the garden's entrance and stroll the fenced area on their own or take a guided tour from a trained docent (by reservation only). Each season offers something new in the garden, be it blooming cherry trees in the early spring, rhododendrons and azaleas throughout the summer, or colored foliage during the fall. Turtles and fish can often be spotted in the landscaped ponds. If you want to see a public tea ceremony, stop by on the third Sunday of any month from April through October. The half-hour narrated demonstration starts at 2 pm and again at 3 pm on these days.

The Japanese Garden is located on Lake Washington Blvd (between E Madison & 23rd Ave S). Admission fee is $2 for adults and $1 for children over six years. Groups are always welcome; special discount rates apply. Hours are 10 am-6 pm or 8 pm; closing time varies according to the season. Call 684-4725 for more information.

Woodland Park & Lower Woodland

N 50th & Phinney N, Aurora N & Green Lake Way N, Seattle

Just east of the Woodland Park Zoo, Woodland Park offers one of the most popular spots in town for big picnics (call 684-4081 to reserve space). With plenty of covered shelters, lots of open space, and close proximity to the zoo and Green Lake, it is a good place to settle for a lazy summer afternoon of barbecuing and frisbee. Soccer, baseball and softball fields and a running track are located at the bottom of the east slope of the park; tennis courts can be found at the south side and down near the soccer fields. To get to Green Lake, take a footbridge over Aurora Ave, and walk across Lower Woodland Park. (See also Woodland Park Zoo in Animals, Animals, Animals and Green Lake in Parks.)

CHAPTER 4

Active Play: Outdoor Fun

Northwest families are eternally optimistic about the great outdoors despite our rainy climate. Indeed, it would be hard not to be, with such spectacular scenery: majestic mountains frame our horizon, cool waters part the landscape, and tall evergreens stand tall against the threat of cement urbanization.

Every season brings a new array of outdoor opportunities for kids, from skiing and sledding, to fishing and hiking. The greater Seattle area boasts many places to boat, bike, skate and ride horses year-round. Don't let a lack of experience or equipment stop you from taking a trip up to the mountains or a bike ride to a scenic picnic spot—many places in the area offer instruction and rentals.

Photo credit:Michael Ziegler

Biking

In the movies, a kid can ride his bike through the sky, past a bright full moon. Large groups of siblings can go cycling through Switzerland, singing and riding in perfect harmony. In Seattle, we don't have all the movie magic, but we do have the Seattle Engineering Department, King County Public Works and the Cascade Bicycle Club. The city and the county have worked with the many avid bicyclists in the area to develop an impressive network of bicycle trails, along with comprehensive maps, highlighting both on- and off-road routes. You can receive a free Seattle Bicycling GuideMap by calling 684-5087, or by going to the Seattle Engineering Department at the Municipal Building in downtown Seattle. The King County Bicycling GuideMap is available at REI stores for about $4. These guides are helpful resources for planning a bicycle outing that accommodates all members of the family.

☆ *Essentials*

If you don't have enough bicycles in the house, or want to avoid the hassle of transporting them, rent

☆ *Tips*

Special family bicycling events are scheduled by various organizations throughout the Puget Sound area, especially during the summer months. The Cascade Bicycle Club (522-BIKE) offers loads of information for novice and experienced bicyclists, as well as classes and group events. Discovery Park in Magnolia offers Bike Hikes with the Ranger—a bike ride and tour around Discovery Park. Call 386-4236 for more information.

From May through September, the Seattle Parks Department designates two weekend days per month as Bicycle Saturdays and Sundays. On these days, with the help of the Seattle Engineering Department, Lake Washington Blvd from Seward Park to Mt. Baker Beach is closed to vehicle traffic between 10 am and 6 pm. Bicycle safety checks and first aid stations are set up along the route.

Whatever bike route you choose, try not to rush it—pack a lunch and take your time. Instead of setting a distance goal, just ride for the fun of it, stopping along the way to relax and unwind.

bikes from one of the following shops. Most have tandem bikes and child carriers available, and all loan helmets of varying sizes (often included in the cost of the bike rental).

Bike Rentals in Seattle:

Alki Bicycle Company, 2611 California SW, 938-3322
Al Young Bike & Ski, 3615 NE 45th, 524-2642
The Bicycle Center, 4529 Sand Point Way NE, 523-8300
Gregg's Greenlake Cycle, 7007 Woodlawn Ave NE, 523-1822
Montlake Bicycle Shop, 2223 24th Ave E, 329-7333
Seattle Sports Exchange, 2232 15th W, 285-4777

On the Eastside:

Bothell Ski & Bike, 17816 Bothell Way NE, Bothell, 486-3747
Montlake Bicycle Shop, 514 Central Way, Kirkland, 828-3800; 10047 Main Street, Bellevue, 462-8823
Redmond Cycle, 16205 Redmond Way, Redmond, 885-6363
Sammamish Valley Cycle, 8451 164th Ave NE, Redmond, 881-8442
Spoke & Ski, 13300 NE 175th, Woodinville, 483-6626

It's a law that children must wear helmets when cycling in unincorporated areas of King County. But make sure everyone wears a helmet, wherever you cycle.

The following routes are off-road pathways, offering a safer ride for youngsters and a more relaxing ride for adults.

Alki

SW Florida St to Lincoln Park, West Seattle
Nearby bike rentals: Alki Bicycle Company, 938-3322
Length one way: 14 miles

One way to enjoy beautiful Alki Beach is to hop on bikes and take this delightful ride along the water around the tip of West Seattle. The trail is safe and wide (about 10 feet) and features a separate six-foot path for pedestrians. The faster riders and racers tend to stay on the roadway, making the bicycle path pretty safe for kids.

Burke Gilman Trail & Sammamish River Trail

Gas Works Park at north Lake Union to Marymoor Park in Redmond
Nearby bike rentals in Seattle: Al Young Bike & Ski, 524-2642; The Bicycle Center, 523-8300
Nearby bike rentals on the Eastside: Bothell Ski & Bike, 486-3747; Redmond Cycle, 885-6363; Sammamish Valley Cycle, 881-8442; Spoke & Ski in Woodinville, 483-6626
Length one way: 25+ miles

With the completion of the connection between the Burke Gilman Trail on the west side of Lake Washington and the Sammamish River Trail on the east side, bicyclists can now enjoy a level, scenic route from Gas Works Park at Lake Union, past the UW, around the north end of Lake Washington through Kenmore, to Marymoor Park in Redmond. Although too far for most young children (and many adults), this route gives riders many shorter options and allows you to start wherever is most convenient. One nice family ride is the 3 1/2-mile stretch from Marymoor Park to the wineries in Woodinville.

The Burke Gilman and Sammamish River trails are flat and paved and are often heavily traveled, especially on weekends. Some of the congestion has been alleviated by the building of the Burke Gilman Alternate Route on the west side of Lake Washington, which is for the more speedy cyclists.

Elliott Bay Bicycle Path

Pier 70, north through Myrtle Edwards Park
Length one way: 1.25 miles

This trail is rarely crowded, although it attracts a large number of downtowners who are trying to get some exercise and fresh air at lunch time. Take the kids on a nice spring or summer evening, stop at the fishing pier and watch the sun set over the water.

Green Lake

Between N 59th & N 77th, just northeast of Woodland Park Zoo
Nearby bike rentals: Gregg's Greenlake Cycle, 523-1822
Length: 2.8-mile loop

The trail around the lake is flat and paved, and there are several playgrounds and grassy areas to stop at along the way. On almost every sunny day, however, the loop gets very crowded with cyclists, joggers, couples, roller skaters, baby strollers and dogs—all going every which way—creating a rather hazardous situation for tikes on trikes or wobbly two-wheelers. It is a more enjoyable, less risky ride on cloudy days or weekday mornings. Just a note: though many of us remember feeding the Green Lake ducks in our younger days, it is no longer permitted.

Green River Trail

S 160th & the Green River to S 200th in Tukwila
Length one way: 2+ miles

The Green River Trail follows the scenic Green River as it winds through the Renton and Kent valleys. A good place to park your car and pick up the trail is at Briscoe Park, situated at one of the bends of the river at S 190th St. From there you can travel north or south along the flat, paved, uncrowded trail. Briscoe Park has picnic areas, a boat launch and play fields as well, so the day can be broken up with several activities if you wish.

Interurban Trail

S 180th St in Tukwila to S 6th & Crow St (a few blocks south of downtown Kent)
Length one way: 4.5+ miles

The Interurban Trail runs underneath Puget Power's power lines and is flat and paved. Parking is available at many sites along the trail, but one of the more convenient places is located at S 180th St, off the West Valley Hwy on the west side of the river. You can pick up the Green River Trail or the Interurban Trail here, or take some time to relax in the park, which has a play area with swings.

Seward Park Loop

East end of Seward Park parking lot, Seattle
Length: 2 1/2-mile loop

This short loop around the outside of Seward Park along Lake Washington is an ideal place for even the wobbliest rider to enjoy fabulous scenery and a flat, easy ride. The trail is a road that has been closed, so it is plenty wide, and it doesn't get crowded on even the busiest summer weekends. The views here are exceptional—Mt. Rainier to the south and the city skyline to the east. Stop at the small fish hatcheries close to the beginning of the trail for a fun break, or have a picnic at one of the many picnic tables along the way. Plan to swim at the lifeguarded beach at the end of your ride if it is a hot day. To get there take Lake Washington Blvd all the way to Seward Park, and drive straight ahead past the main entrance. Then take a left and park at the end of the parking lot.

Soos Creek Trail

SE 208th St & 136th Ave SE in Kent, south to SE 264th St & 150th Ave SE (a few blocks east of Lake Meridian)
Length one way: 4+ miles

This is a scenic, paved trail along Soos Creek, east of Kent. Parking is available at the trail's north end at SE 208th and 136th Ave SE, where families can take advantage of a park and picnic area. The route is mostly flat, especially at the north end, and is divided for horse and bike traffic. It is not heavily traveled.

Boating

You'd think, with the amount of rain we get, that Northwesterners would be sick of water. Instead it's quite the opposite: about one out of every 23 people in Washington owns a boat. Boating is a wonderful family activity, providing your child isn't chronically stir-crazy. Most kids are thrilled to sit in a small boat dragging a stick or a toy boat on a string, trying their hand at paddling and just watching other boats go by.

☆ *Essentials*

Boating, like any water sport, can also be dangerous, so take proper precautions before you push off the shore: Check the weather conditions, and make sure everyone, even the best swimmer, is wearing a PFD (Personal Flotation Device—the latest, hippest name yet for life vest). Also, never let a child go out in a boat without an adult.

When you are out on the water in the summertime, protect your skin and eyes. Even if the sky is overcast, be sure that everybody uses sunscreen and wears hats and sunglasses.

☆ *Tips*

Although boat rental places are required to provide life vests, to be safe bring along your child's own life vest when you rent a boat. That way you will know you have the best fit and style for your child's age and size.

At the Center for Wooden Boats' Festival held on the Fourth of July weekend, children enjoy activities designed to teach maritime skills.

Photo credit: The Center for Wooden Boats

The Center for Wooden Boats
1010 Valley St, Seattle
382-BOAT (2628)
Open year-round 12-6 pm; closed Tuesday
Rentals available starting at $8/hour
Life vests provided

With an interesting shoreline of houseboats and sea planes from Lake Union Air taking off and landing frequently, Lake Union is a fun place to rent boats. The Center for Wooden Boats, located on the south end of Lake Union, offers rowing, paddling and sailing craft for rental year-round. Before being allowed to rent sailing craft, the customer's boat handling skills will be checked out. The cost to rent sailing craft starts at $10 per hour; rowing and paddling crafts cost $8-$12 per hour. Families memberships to the Center for Wooden Boats are available for $40 and sailing lessons are offered.

☆ *Tips*
Gas Works Park, directly across on the north side of Lake Union, is a good place to get out and let kids stretch their legs at the playground. Further east of this park, before the University Bridge, is Ivar's Salmon House. Pull up to the dock and send someone up to the outside fish bar for tasty fish and chips.

Greenlake Boat Rentals

7351 E Green Lake Dr N, Seattle
527-0171
Rates range from $6-$12 per hour
Life vests provided

Greenlake Boat Rentals, located near the Green Lake Community Center, offers rowboats, paddleboats, canoes or sailboards for rental from mid-April through September. Kids love to navigate their way to the lake's Duck Island, though it's better not explored on foot—too wet and muddy. Boat reservations, though not necessary, are recommended during the summer months.

> ☆ ***Tips***
>
> *There is a reason why Green Lake is so green: algae. During the summer months when the algae is thickest, swimming is not advised. Therefore, if you go on a really hot day, make sure that the breeze is sufficient enough to keep you cool and plan to let the kids splash around in Green Lake park's wading pool.*

Northwest Outdoor Center

2100 Westlake Ave N, Seattle
281-9694
$9/hour per kayak
Life vests provided

Rent a two-person kayak from Northwest Outdoor Center and see Lake Union from a new perspective. Paddle to Gas Works Park in 10 minutes, the Ballard Locks in about 45 minutes. Several different models are available for rental, seating one, two or three people. Kids sit in front, adults in the rear steering position. Rentals are available by the hour, half-day, full day and longer. No experience is necessary.

University of Washington Waterfront Activity Center

University of Washington, south of Husky Stadium
543-9433
Open Feb-Oct, 9 am-dusk
$3.50/hour per boat with driver's license
Life vests provided

Enjoy a leisurely paddle through the Arboretum in a canoe or rowboat rented at the Canoe House. The Foster Island area is full of mysterious byways and foot bridges to navigate through and under, a multitude of interesting birds to observe and unlimited places to hop ashore and stretch. Canoes seat up to three people, and rowboats seat up to four people. Life vests are available for children as small as 25 pounds. Boats are available on a first-come, first-served basis.

Fishing/Clamming/ Musseling

Shellfish

Since kids typically like any activity that allows them to play in wet muck, they quickly catch on to the fun of digging for butter clams and harvesting oysters and mussels off rocks. What's surprising, given the slippery texture of shellfish, is that most kids like eating them, too.

All you'll need for your excursion is a shovel, a bucket, boots (if you don't want wet feet) and a low tide. Seattle's public beaches are open for clamming year-round, unless pollution alerts are posted. Alki Beach is the most popular in-city spot, but digging is better (and the clams are probably healthier) at public beaches in Edmonds and Mukilteo and on Whidbey Island. No license is required unless you're digging for razor clams out on the ocean beaches.

Harvesting mussels is remarkably simple; you just find a large mussel bed (Whidbey Island has many good spots) and pull them off of the rocks. Oysters beds are a bit more scarce.

Clamming seasons are sometimes canceled because of shortages; consult the Department of Fisheries (in Olympia, 206-902-2250) for up-to-date information. There is also a danger of shellfish poisoning from a microscopic organism that can turn the ocean water red (called "red tide"). It is a highly toxic organism for humans that even cooking cannot eliminate, so always call the Red Tide Hotline (800-562-5632) before you take the family shell fishing.

Fishing

Kids 14 and under can fish in Washington anytime, on any public dock in the area, without a license. Others must obtain licenses. For information on fresh water fishing licenses and regulations, call the Washington State Wildlife Department at 206-753-5719; for salt water fishing licenses and regulations, call the Washington State Fisheries Department at 206-902-2464. Most Fred Meyer, Payless, K-Mart, Big Five and Ernst stores sell the licenses and offer booklets covering seasonal regulations.

The following are some popular, public access spots:

Green Lake

Fish anywhere on the lake or at any of the following three piers: northeast corner of the ball field (juveniles only); northwest corner near Duck Island; or southwest corner by the canoe house.

Lake Washington

This lake is home to over 25 species of fish, but most people who dangle a line here are hoping to pull out salmon, steelhead and cutthroat trout. Public fishing access is at the docks listed below.

In Seattle:

Madison Park (at the end of East Madison)
South of Madrona Beach (near the foot of E Jefferson)
Mount Baker Park
North Leschi Moorage (on Lakeside S and Alder E)
S McClellan and 35th S
Seward Park (at Lake Washington Blvd and S Juneau)
Washington Park Arboretum (on the Waterfront Trail)

In Bellevue:
Entai (underneath the I-90 Bridge. Take Bellevue Way exit, turn left on 113th Ave NE)
In Bothell:
Logboom Park (from Bothell Way, south on 61st Ave NE)
In Kirkland:
Wavery Park (on Lake Washington Blvd)
Marina Park (in downtown Kirkland at the foot of Central Way NE)
On Mercer Island:
Luther Burbank Park

Puget Sound

Public fishing is popular at Waterfront Park at the end of Pier 57; the public seawall just north of Pier 70; and off Myrtle Edward's Park at Pier 86. Pier 86 is the most user-friendly spot, with covered areas to take shelter from bad weather and its own bait and tackle shop, the Happy Hooker (you can get snacks and souvenirs here, too). You can also fish at the Alki breakwater and from the pier at the south end of Golden Gardens Park. The pier at Mukilteo next to the ferry dock is an especially good fishing spot, if you want a change of scenery.

Trout Farms

Fishing at a trout farm may not paint the most realistic picture of what this sport is all about, but face it: your child will have plenty of opportunities later in life to experience fishing and catching nothing. The ponds are so crammed the trout seem to want to grab the hooks just to escape the crowded conditions. The only down side of these ventures is that most proud fisherpersons will expect their catch to be eaten and these warm-water fish aren't very tasty.

Some trout farms are seasonal, others are open year-round on a limited schedule. Visitors are charged only for the fish they catch (either by the inch or the pound); all gear, bait and cleaning is included. No licenses are required. Groups are welcome by reservation.

A Lil' Bit O' Heaven, 16636 NE 40th St, Redmond, 883-1654
Cran-Mar Trout Farm, 28633 216th SE, Kent, 630-4912
Gold Creek Trout Farm, 15844 148th Ave NE, Woodinville, 483-1415
Springbrook Trout Farm, 19225 Talbot Rd S, Renton, 852-0360

Hiking

When you think of hiking, do you picture the family in lederhosen, yodeling together upon a mountain peak? Or do you imagine yourself dropping a trail of jellybeans just to get your kids up the hill. Maybe the second scenario is a bit more realistic, but don't get discouraged. Washington is an ideal place for hiking, and once you convince the kids that "walking around the woods" is not a dreadful bore, you may find that you've found a new family activity. Start out with an easy day hike through one of the clubs listed here. It's a great getaway from the phone, the TV and the hassles of the city.

Geology Adventures
255-6635

This interesting organization offers hikes that teach about the geology of the Issaquah area. The adventures are especially geared to parents and kids, and the guides provide a wealth of information, as well as hands-on activities, including gold panning and fossil hunting. Call for details.

Issaquah Alps Trails Club
24-hour hotline: 328-0480

This club's members lead free hikes for all ages and skill levels year-round on the mountains and plateaus in the greater Issaquah area (Tiger, Squak, Cougar, Grand Ridge, Rattlesnake and Taylor). No reservations are necessary and no special gear is required. Each hike is rated by length and climbing difficulty, giving hikers a good idea if it is appropriate for their children. Hikers meet at the Issaquah City Hall at an appointed time, and carpool to the trailhead. Call the Issaquah Alps Hotline above for a complete hike schedule and more information.

The Mountaineers
284-6310

The Mountaineers is the largest outdoor organization in the region, currently comprising 14,000 members. The club is dedicated to offering a wide array of outdoor activities for all ages, including hiking, cross-country skiing, backpack trips, kayaking and more. Several memberships are available including individual, spouse and junior. In addition, Mountaineer Books publishes two excellent guides for families that want to hike together: *Best Hikes With Children in Western Washington & the Cascades*, volumes 1 & 2. These guides are available at local bookstores or by contacting the Mountaineers.

Horseback Riding

Does your child sleep with a hobby horse and wear cowboy boots to bed? Do you trip over little plastic horses whenever you enter your daughter's room? Horseback riding is a real thrill for young horse lovers, and all of the places listed below provide trail rides and, in some cases, riding classes, summer day camps and overnight camps. Call for details on classes and camps.

Aqua Barn Ranch
15227 SE Renton-Maple Valley Hwy, Renton
255-4618, 800-284-2227
Trail rides $8/hr

This ranch offers instructional guided trail rides by reservation only. Anyone over eight years old can participate in the trail ride; kids under eight can ride a parent-led pony for about 15 minutes for $4.

High Country Outfitters
3020 Issaquah Pine Lake Rd, Suite 544, Issaquah
392-0111
Packages start at $110/day

This organization offers a variety of trail ride packages, varying in length and difficulty. You choose from guided day rides to extended pack trips into the Wenatchee National Forest and Alpine Lakes Wilderness areas. They also operate Camp Wahoo, an accredited resident camp for children, and Red Gate Farm Day Camp in Issaquah, a summer day camp. Reservations are required.

Horse Country
8507 Hwy 92, Granite Falls
691-7509
Trail rides $15/hr

Horse Country features trail rides for everyone from five-year-olds to grandparents. One hour and 1 1/2 hour rides are offered. Reservations required.

Kelly's Ranch
7212 Renton-Issaquah Rd, Issaquah
392-6979
Trail rides $8-$10/half hour

Open year-round, this ranch offers hour-long guided trail rides for $20 per person, seven days a week. Children as young as four years can participate, or parents can lead youngsters around the property for about $8 per half-hour. Experienced guides will do the same for $10 per half-hour. Reservations are requested.

Lake Serene Pony Farm
3915 Serene Way, Lynnwood
743-2112
Trail rides $10/45 minutes

Located just north of Lynnwood, this beautiful farm offers riding lessons for children preschool age and up. Forty-five minute trail rides are available on Saturdays during the spring, summer and fall months for about $10; preschoolers can ride for approximately 15 minutes on a parent-led pony for $4. During the summer months, week-long day camps are offered for children six-14 years to teach trail riding, arena riding and care and feeding of the horses. Reservations required.

Little Bit Therapeutic Riding Center
19802 NE 148th, Woodinville
882-1554

This non-profit organization offers therapeutic horseback riding programs for differently-abled persons, emphasizing their capabilities, rather than their limitations.

Tiger Mountain Outfitters
24508 SE 133rd, Issaquah
392-5090
$40 per person

Tiger Mountain Outfitters offers trail rides year-round for anyone over 10 years of age. Call ahead for reservations, and they will take you on a three-hour guided ride through 14,000 acres on Tiger Mountain.

Mini Golf (Outdoor)

Dress your children in green plaid pants and Izod cardigans, and teach them what the good life is all about.

Green Lake Pitch 'n Putt

5701 W Green Lake Way N, Seattle
632-2280
Greens fees are $3-$4;
club rentals, $.50/person; balls, $.75-$1

If you want to introduce your older child to the real game of golf, this is the place. Green Lake Pitch 'n Putt is not a minigolf course; it's a nine hole, par 3 course on eight acres on Green Lake's south shore. The course is open April through October, with holes ranging from 55 to 115 yards. You can bring your own clubs and balls or rent them.

Jazwieck's Golf & Train

7828 Broadway, Everett
355-5646
18 holes, $3.75; train ride $3.50

Jazwieck's outdoor amusement park is open during the spring, summer and fall, weather permitting, and features a miniature 18-hole lighted putting course, as well as a miniature train that runs along 2,000 feet of track. The 15-minute train ride includes a trip through the woods, past carved animals, dolls and mini versions of Mt. Rushmore and the Statue of Liberty. The train operates on a limted schedule during summer months, so be sure to call to check if it is running unless you plan to just play golf. Tickets for the train ride and miniature course are sold separately.

Riverbend Mini Putt-Putt

2020 West Meeker, Kent
859-4000
$2/children; $3/adults

Riverbend is an outdoor 18-hole miniature course open daily year-round. Groups and birthday celebrations are also welcome with advance reservations.

River Rafting

With an abundance of beautiful rivers, it is no wonder that river rafting is a popular sport in the Northwest. For families, a guided river rafting trip is an expensive but unforgettable experience. There are two types of river rafting: white-water, which is through rapids and full of thrills (and potential spills) and the serene float trips, when the raft meanders downstream. Both types usually offer magnificent scenery, wildlife viewing and a fascinating up-close look at the river.

Most rafting companies will not take kids under the age of six for safety reasons. School-age kids typically love river rafting, especially if the trip includes both mild rapids and interesting wildlife. The Methow, Skykomish and Wenatchee rivers are recommended in the late spring and summer; in the winter, Skagit River bald eagle float trips are very popular with families.

There are many good river rafting companies in this region. Most are very helpful in recommending good river runs that will suit the age range in your group. Most also provide food if you so desire. Be sure to ask if they have price discounts for kids or large groups.

Here are some of the most popular rafting companies:

Downstream River Runners, 12112 NE 195th St, Bothell, 483-0335
Northern Wilderness River Riders, 23312 77th Ave SE, Woodinville, 448-RAFT
Zig Zag Expeditions, 180 Nickerson, Seattle, 282-2840

Outdoor Roller Skating

Outdoor skating, whether in-line or the old-fashioned way, is somewhat trickier than skating in an indoor rink, because there are curbs, slopes and rough surfaces to negotiate. It helps to have at least one steady adult that can be leaned on. In-line skates, with their single blade of wheels, may look daunting, but both adults and children will find them easier to use than the old four-wheelers.

Call the In-Line Infoline (528-2508) for information on upcoming events, instruction, skate rentals and good places to skate.

☆ *Tips*

Do not attempt a skating adventure on a popular trail on a sunny day until all your skaters have developed good balance and control. Instead, practice on the sidewalk or at a playground. If you have a baby stroller, put some phonebooks (or a willing little sister or brother) in it and let the beginning skater push it along while she learns.

☆ *Essentials*

Rentals in Seattle are available at Gregg's Greenlake Cycle, 523-1822. Be sure that you and your kids wear the pads that come free with the rental. During the summer months, you can usually find a mobile skate rental shop out at Alki as well.

Snow Fun

Seattle families are lucky to be able to jump into their cars on a winter weekend and arrive at the mountains within an hour. There are plenty of opportunities for you and your kids to have snow fun without enormous expense. Remember to dress kids well so they stay warm and dry, carry chains at all times, bring plenty of snacks, and call the Washington State Department of Transportation Pass Information line (Nov-Apr), at 455-7900, to check on road and weather conditions before you venture forth.

Tubing and Sledding

Snow Flake Tubing & Snow Play

Snoqualmie Pass, east corner of Ski Acres parking lot
285-TUBE
Admission $5.50/person (under 5 free); tube rental $4.50

Snow Flake is a gentle slope open Friday through Monday during the ski season for tubers and sledders only. Kids rent or bring their own inner tubes, and have the option to take a rope tow up the hill (ticket required). There is also a small area for sledding, though sleds are not

☆ ***Tips***

Snow Flake hill gets crowded on weekends and may be daunting to a preschooler. The advantage of bringing your own sleds or saucers is that you can find small hills in the area that are free, and usually less crowded. (Along the road to the Alpental ski area, there are several good spots for sledding. To get there take a left turn after you exit for the Snoqualmie Ski area and follow signs to Alpental.)

for rent. Admission is charged whether or not you bring your own tube.

☆ ***Essentials***

The Snow Flake area has a snack bar and restrooms.

Cross Country Skiing

Ski Acres Cross-Country Center
434-6646 *or* 232-8182
Stevens Pass Nordic Center
973-2441

The ski areas at Snoqualmie Pass (Ski Acres and Hyak) and Stevens Pass offer groomed trails for cross-country skiers of all abilities. Skiers can purchase a Sno-Park permit which entitles them to park at designated lots on the mountain. With your permit, which is available at REI stores, Wilderness Sports in Bellevue (746-0500), Swallow's Nest in Seattle (441-4100) and other outdoor retail stores, you will receive a map of the trail locations. You may also purchase a booklet that describes the trails and facilities. Good cross-country trails are also plentiful in the Leavenworth area.

☆ ***Essentials***

Equipment rentals for cross-country skiing are available at several outdoor retail stores in Seattle, including REI and Swallow's Nest.

Check out Ski Acres Cross Country Ski School under Ski Classes, if you are interested in lessons for the kids.

Downhill Skiing

Snoqualmie and Ski Acres are the two best areas for beginning skiers. They have several bunny hills and lifts that give novices a chance to get steady on their skis before facing steeper slopes. All the areas offer family discount season passes that provide significant savings. Prices vary depending on day of the week and time of day you ski.

All the areas also offer private lessons and rental equipment (skis, boots and poles) for the day, so let your kids try it out before you invest further in season lessons and equipment.

Ski Classes for Kids

Many organizations in the Seattle area offer ski lessons for children as well as adults, some accepting students as young as two or three years old. Although most ski schools don't begin classes until the first two weeks of January, register early for best class selection. Some organizations also offer snowboarding lessons for older children and teens. Prices for these programs vary, depending on the number of classes, day of the week and age of the student. Call the phone numbers listed to receive program brochures.

If you want to give your child one or two lessons without investing in a season of lessons and lift tickets, all of the ski areas near Seattle give private and semi-private lessons. Ski equipment can also be rented for a day at all areas.

If your child is interested in skiing, but you don't want to invest in equipment that will be quickly outgrown, many area ski shops (Olympic Sports, Al Young Bike & Ski and Mini-Mountain Indoor Ski School, for example) offer the option of renting or leasing ski equipment for the season.

Alpental Ski School

Alpental
434-6364
Private and semi-private lessons for ages 3 through adult

Classes here are offered in five- and eight-week sessions during the ski season. Holiday Ski Camps for children ages six and up, featuring games, exercises and plenty of ski time, are offered in December. Buddy Werner Racing Team classes are also offered for children ages eight-12 years, which combine basic skiing and racing skills. Transportation via chartered bus from Seattle or Bellevue is available; children under age eight must be accompanied by an adult.

Audett's Ski King Ski School

Stevens Pass
822-3522
Lessons for ages 6 through adult

Audett's lessons are sold in six- or eight-week packages. Transportation packages to and from the mountain are also available.

Bob Hall Ski School

Stevens Pass
746-2451
Lessons for ages 4 1/2 through adult

This ski school offers a variety of eight-week sessions, including half- and full-day instruction, as well as Friday evening classes. Transportation packages are also available.

Crystal Mountain Ski School

Crystal Mountain
663-2265
Lessons for children ages 4 through adult

Drop-in lessons are available daily throughout the ski season, as are discount packages that entitle the bearer to take lessons at their convenience. For first-time skiers, packages are offered that include one or two lessons on the same day, rental equipment and lift ticket. Child care is available on weekdays by reservation for infants and children ages two to seven.

Fiorini Ski School

Snoqualmie Pass
Lessons for ages 5-15 years
Crystal Mountain
Lessons for ages 12-15 years with advanced skills
722-6800

All Fiorini lessons are sold in eight-week packages, and can include transportation for ages six and up. For more information, visit Fiorini Sports in the University Village or call the above number.

Mini-Mountain Indoor Ski School

1900 132nd Ave NE, Bellevue
746-7547
10700 5th Ave NE, Seattle
363-2019 (located inside Olympic Sports)
Private and semi-private classes for ages 2 1/2 through adult

This indoor school provides all lesson equipment. Programs include half-hour lessons, Skirobics for pre-season conditioning and an on-snow ski school at Snoqualmie, as well as equipment rental and lease.

Mogul Mouse Ski School

Snoqualmie
283-2835
Lessons for children ages 4 and up, from beginner to advanced

Mogul Mouse's classes are small, and lessons for Mini Mice (four-year-olds) include helmet rental for the season. Private lessons are also available.

Norski Ski School

Stevens Pass
392-7600
Lessons for children ages 6 and up (classes for children as young as 4 years are also offered on a one-on-one basis)

Norski offers Friday evening and Sunday packages (transportation packages available on Sundays). "Flex Time" offers skiers the opportunity to purchase unlimited lesson coupons to use at their discretion—create your own lesson schedule.

Olympic Ski School

Stevens Pass
483-2484
Lessons for ages 4 through adult

Olympic boasts the largest Small Fry Program at Stevens Pass. Classes are held on weekends, Saturday or Sunday, for eight weeks. Transportation packages are also available.

Powderpigs Children's Ski School

Ski Acres
392-7277
Lessons for children ages 3 and up

Classes at Powderpigs are scheduled both mid-week and weekends. Tuition includes lessons, a red ski school parka with Powderpigs patch and a blue wool hat. The hats and parkas are worn by all instructors and students.

Seattle Times Ski School

Alpental, Ski Acres, Snoqualmie and Hyak
236-7226
Lesson for ages 4 through adult, beginner through advanced

The Times' classes are scheduled on a variety of days and evenings to fit every need. Snowboarding classes are offered for ages 12 through adult.

Ski Acres Cross-Country Ski School

Ski Acres
232-8182
Lessons for ages 4 through adult

If you want your child to try out this popular style of skiing before signing up for lessons, try the drop-in classes or private lessons. Classes fill up quickly, so register early.

Ski Acres Ski School

Ski Acres
823-2690
Lessons for ages 5 through adult

Drop-in, private, group and snowboarding classes are available through this school. Skiers may also purchase "flex" packages of five lessons each, to be used at their convenience throughout the season.

Ski-attle Ski School

Snoqualmie
364-4952
Lessons for students in 2nd-12th grades

This program, presented by the Seattle Council PTSA, offers equipment rental packages as well as transportation packages. Classes are offered for all skill levels on Friday evenings, Saturdays and Sundays. Snowboarding lessons are also available for teenagers.

Skiforall School & Foundation

Snoqualmie, Ski Acres and Hyak
328-3732
Lessons for children ages 5 and up

Skiforall offers recreation programs for people with disabilities. Cross country and downhill lessons include all adaptive equipment, and financial aid is available. Transportation is also offered on Saturday and Sunday.

Ski Klasses, Inc.

Stevens Pass
774-3259
Lessons for children ages 5 and up

Ski Klasses' all-day instruction includes two hours in the morning and two hours in the afternoon. Transportation is also available.

SkiMasters Ski School

Snoqualmie
451-8228
Lessons for children ages 4 and up

SkiMasters holds classes on weekends, and has its own chalet where kids can go to warm up, dry clothes or just rest. House Mothers are on staff all day to help. Eight-week half-day and full-day programs are available, as well as transportation packages on Saturday and Sunday from several locations in Seattle and Bellevue, including the Bainbridge Island Ferry Terminal. Stop by Sturtevant Sports in Bellevue for information and registration, or call either of the numbers above.

Snoqualmie Ski Program

Snoqualmie
434-6363
Lessons for children ages 3 and up

This program operates Tuesday through Sunday. Drop-in classes and series classes are offered, as well as round-trip transportation from several locations in Seattle, Bellevue and Issaquah. A beginner package is offered for first-time skiers, which includes one lesson (group or private), equipment rental and lift ticket.

Star Skiers

Crystal Mountain
392-8550
Lessons for children ages 4 and up

In addition to beginner skiing lessons, Star Skiers boasts a very successful Mitey Mite Program for children six years and up at the intermediate ski level. Instruction stresses responsibility on the mountain, ski safety and socialization skills. Lessons are offered on weekend days in three-, six-, eight- and nine-week packages. Transportation packages are available from Mercer Island.

CHAPTER 5

Active Play: Indoor Fun

The mid-January post holiday crash has hit. Or maybe summer vacation started a week ago and it hasn't stopped raining since the last school bell rang. The kids are swinging from the light fixtures.

You can't face another craft project—now what? Let them ride in cardboard boxes down the basement stairs? Insist the little critters clean their closets? Cruise the malls? How about recruiting another family for some sanity-preserving adult company and trying out one of these energy-burning activities.

Bowling

Bellevue Square Boat

First Floor, Bellevue Square
454-4340 or 454-8096
Hours: Mon-Sat, 9:30 am-9:30 pm; Sun, 11 am-6 pm
Free admission

Known simply as the Boat, this tot attraction in the heart of Bellevue Square offers lots of climbing fun for toddlers and preschoolers. Kids just love, in fact beg, to stop and play on this padded little tugboat. The boat is completely encircled by a carpeted bench where parents can sit, relax and scheme about how they are going to manage to get their kids off the thing and back to shopping. The Boat is restricted to children under six years of age.

Bumper Bowling

BCA (Sportsworld), 27403 Pacific Hwy S, Kent, 941-4700
Brunswick Majestic Lanes, 1300 164th SW, Lynnwood, 743-4422
Cascade Lanes, 17034 116th SE, Renton, 226-2035
Imperial Lanes, 2101 22nd S, Seattle, 325-2525
Kent Bowl, 1234 N Central, Kent, 852-3550
Leilani Lanes, 10201 Greenwood N, Seattle, 783-8010
Lynnwood Lanes, 6210 200th SW, Lynnwood, 778-3133
Person Lanes, 1905 Howard Rd, Auburn, 833-4146
Robin Hood Lanes, 9801 Edmonds Way, Edmonds, 776-2101
Roxbury Lanes, 2823 SW Roxbury St, West Seattle, 935-7400
Sun Villa Lanes, Eastgate Shopping Center, Bellevue, 455-8155

> ☆ **Tips**
> *It is a good idea to call the bowling alley in advance to make sure there will be bumper lanes available. And once you get there, refrain from trying to explain the scoring system to a group of kids under age 10. Just handle the scorekeeping yourself, unless you are a glutton for punishment.*

Get the convertible Chevy out, give the kids some Bazooka and throw Elvis on the 8-track. It's family bowling night, but with a twist: bumpers. No more tears over the fated gutter ball—these gutter pads will guide your child's bowling ball straight to the Big Ten, ensurring at least one satisfying crash. Beware, of course, of the other, not-so-good crashes, like Bowling Ball On the Toe, Child and Attached Bowling Ball Bouncing Down the Lane, and Bowling Ball Hurled Backwards Toward Little Sister.

Bumper bowling is gaining popularity (partially because it helps parents avoid embarrassment, too). Prices vary a bit from alley to alley, usually about $2-$3 per game plus the shoe rental (about $1-$2, complete with Velcro). If you can't find shoes small enough to fit your kids, they can bowl in their socks (adds slippery thrills). The bowling alleys listed above offer bumper bowling on select days during daytime hours on a first-come first-served basis. Most others offer bumper bowling by reservation.

Ice Skating

Highland Ice Arena
18005 Aurora Ave N, Seattle
546-2431
Open daily year-round; public skate sessions vary
$3/children ages 6-11; $4/adults; $1.50 skate rental

Sno-King Ice Arena
19803 68th Ave W, Lynnwood
775-7511
Open daily year-round; public skate sessions vary
$4/person; select 'Cheap Skate' events $2.50; skate rental $2

Most youngsters more or less crawl around the rink on their first few ice skating attempts, so be sure to provide mittens and encourage plenty of breaks for hot chocolate. Also, you might mention to the kids that though Olympic skaters make it look really easy, they had to sweat for six hours a day beginning at 4 am for most of their childhood to become so graceful on those skinny blades. It also helps to bring along at least one adult who has enough control on the ice to remain upright despite flailing kids hanging onto him.

> ☆ ***Tips***
> *If you're lucky (or you call ahead), you might catch a curling match at an adjacent ice rink. This bizarre Scottish sport, which is played with brooms, is always fun to watch.*

Indoor Playgrounds

Indoor playgrounds have sprung up all over the Seattle area in the last few years and no wonder. Northwest parents have been starved for places to let kids burn off excess energy on those too-wet-to-go-out days. At these brightly colored playgrounds, kids 12 and under can climb, jump, slide, bounce, balance and more in tubes, tunnels, ball baths, obstacle courses and slides. Highly energetic parents can join in the fun for free or sit back and have a cup of coffee and a snack from the snack bar. At certain playgrounds, parents may rent a beeper and go off for their own fun for a couple of hours.

At the indoor playgrounds listed below:

*There are separate areas for toddlers and preschoolers, so little ones don't get run over by stampeding nine-year-olds.
*Birthday parties and group events are available. (Reserve space early because they fill up fast.)
*Special passes for frequent users are offered.
*Socks are required.
*Accompanying adults play free
*Parents are required to stay on the premises EXCEPT at Playspace and Tube Town.

City Park
20510 108th SE, Kent
850-7529
Hours: Mon-Sat, 9 am-9 pm; Sun, 10 am-7 pm
$5.49/child

Discovery Zone
1130 SE Everett Mall Way, Everett
290-8325
Hours: Mon, 12-9 pm; Tues-Sat, 10 am-9 pm; Sun, 11 am- 6 pm
$5.25/child

Energy Cube
12035 124th Ave NE, Kirkland
820-KIDS (5437)
Hours: Mon-Sat, 9 am-9 pm; Sun, 10 am-6 pm
$5.50/child
Offers drop-in aerobics classes for adults while their kids play and gymnastic classes for kids.

Energy Zone Bellevue (formerly Discovery Zone)
14506 NE 20th, Bellevue
643-2550
Hours: Mon, 12-8 pm; Tues-Fri, 10 am-8 pm; Sat, 9:30 am-9:30 pm; Sun 11 am-6 pm
$5.49/child Energy Zone Lake Forest Park (formerly Discovery Zone)

Energy Zone Lake Forest Park (formerly Discovery Zone)
17171 Bothell Way NE, Seattle; 363-4844
Hours: Mon, 12-8 pm; Tues-Fri, 10 am-8 pm; Sat, 9:30 am-9:30 pm; Sun, 11 am-6 pm
$5.25/child

Play Club
19723 Hwy 99, Suite F, Lynnwood
778-4009
Hours: Sun-Mon, 11 am-7 pm; Tues-Thurs, 9:30 am-8 pm; Fri-Sat, 9:30 am-9 pm
$4.75/first child; Mon-Fri, five or more children, $4.25/each additional child

Playspace
156th Ave NE & NE 8th St, Bellevue; Crossroads Shopping Center
644-4500
Hours: Mon-Thurs, 9 am-9 pm; Fri-Sat, 9 am-10:30 pm; Sun, 10 am-6 pm
$5.95/child
Drop-off care is also available for $5.95/hour (plus $1 for a pager). Every Friday and Saturday night, Playspace offers Parents Night Out, an evening of child care for ages 3-12, which includes a movie, dinner, craft, storytime, play time in the tunnel tubes, and a pager for the parents. Cost of Parents Night Out is $16.50/child.

Tube Town
Located in Factoria Square Mall
747-2020
Hours: Mon-Fri, 10 am-8 pm; Sat, 10 am-6 pm; Sun, 12-5 pm
$5.55/child
Offers drop-in child care for ages 3-11 ($5.50/child per hour). Also offers special rates for groups who wish to hold weekly play group sessions at Tube Town, and provides assistance in finding a play group. Parents Paradise on Saturday night provides child care from 6:30-10:30 pm ($16/child).

Indoor Playgrounds for Toddlers & Preschoolers

Bellevue Parks Department, 455-7686
Green Lake Community Center, Seattle, 684-0780
Kent Parks Department, 859-3350
King County Parks Northshore/ Shoreline District, 296-2976
Kirkland Parks Department, 828-1217

Several parks departments in the Seattle and Eastside areas offer drop-in indoor playgrounds for toddlers and preschoolers. Some programs are offered year-round, others only during the school year or select winter months. Special play equipment is set up for these regularly scheduled programs, including climbing apparatus, mats, balls, trikes, toys and tunnels to offer children some energy burning fun. Adults must accompany the children at all times. The fee for admission is nominal, usually about $1 per child. The schedules and equipment vary for each location; call the site nearest you for details.

☆ Tips

Parenting a young child is often a very lonely experience, expecially when the wet weather keeps everybody inside. The indoor playgrounds for toddlers and preschoolers give parents a chance to get to know other parents in the neighborhood.

Indoor Family Entertainment Centers

The atmosphere is "indoor carnival"— noisy, crowded and fun. The gazillion video games could captivate your kids for hours, but don't let them miss out on other activities available, such as Lazer Tag, batting cages, bumper cars, mini-golf and go-karts. Not all the centers have the same attractions, but they all have more than enough to keep older kids (6 and up) busy for several hours. Seattle Funplex and Games have redemption skill games, where players can receive small prizes (candy, baseball cards, etc.) for high scores—making the tests of strength and agility all the more exciting.

☆ *Essentials*

Admission is not charged at these facilities. Instead, you buy tickets and tokens for various activities and packaged deals. Expect to spend at least $10 per person, excluding food.

All of these places have snack bars with pizza, hot dogs, popcorn, etc.

Funtasia Family Sports & Entertainment

7212 220th St SW, Edmonds
774-GAME
Sun-Thurs, 11 am-11 pm; Fri, 11 am-2 am; Sat, 10 am-2 am

Games

3616 S Road, Mukilteo
353-6800
Sun-Thurs, 11 am-10 pm; Fri-Sat, 11 am-midnight

☆ ***Tips***

All these centers (except Games) have a toddler area with preschool games, however they are best suited for older children and teens. Place the average preschooler in this over-stimulating environment and his mood will likely deteriorate from frantic glee to sensory overload with a nasty short circuit into tears within the first 30 minutes.

The centers don't require that kids be accompanied by an adult, but it would not be appropriate to leave a younger child (under age 10) unattended. There are plenty of helpful employees, but they are not babysitters—and the centers are large and usually crowded.

Zones has teen dances on Saturday nights ($6 cover).

Weekends and school vacations are busiest; try to take kids at a slow time for the most fun.

Seattle Funplex Indoor Amusement Park
1541 15th Ave W, Seattle
285-7842
Sun-Thurs, 11 am-10 pm; Fri, 11 am-1 am; Sat, 10 am-1 am

Zones
2207 Bellevue-Redmond Rd, Redmond; located just east of Sears
746-9411
Mon-Thurs, 11 am-9 pm; Fri-Sat, 11 am-midnight; Sun, 12-8 pm

Roller Skating

Skate King
2301 140th Ave NE, Bellevue, 641-2046
10210 SE 260th, Kent, 852-9371
Skate sessions vary; call for schedule
$2.50-$4/person, cash only; skate rental $1.25

Roll-a-Way Skate Center
6210 200th SW, Lynnwood, 778-4446
Skate sessions vary; call for schedule
$2.25-$3.75, cash or checks only; skate rental $1.50

Yes—they still do the Hokey Pokey, and they still play the Top Forty. But don't let your warped, disco-days memories stop you from taking the kids roller skating. Not only is it easier than ice skating, it's much warmer. Skaters can bring their own skates (not in-lines if they have been worn outside) or rent skates at the rink. Rates vary depending on day and time. Activities for families include family skate sessions with special rates, tiny tot skates, teen skates,

Photo credit: Roberta Wilkes

drop-in skate lessons and special birthday party packages.

Swimming

An indoor swim in the middle of winter soothes hyper kids and gives parents a chance to sneak in a few laps. The public pools in the area have designated family swim times, and the admission fee is very reasonable.

All the pools listed below are indoors (except where noted) and all offer family swims and lessons.

Seattle Parks and Recreation Pools

Cost of admission is $2 for adults and $1.25 for ages 1 to 18. Swim tickets are also available for further savings.

Ballard, 1471 NW 67th, 684-4094
Evans, 7201 E Green Lake Dr N, 684-4961
Helene Madison, 13401 Meridian N, 684-4979
Meadowbrook, 10515 35th NE, 684-4989
Medgar Evers, 500 23rd, 684-4766
Queen Anne, 1920 1st W, 386-4282
Rainier Beach, 8825 Rainier S, 386-1944
Southwest, 2801 SW Thistle, 684-7440
(Colman Pool in Lincoln Park is an outdoor, saltwater heated pool open during summer months only. See Parks.)

King County Pools

Cost of admission during a family swim session is $1.25 per person at the King County Pools. Call the pool closest to you for family swim information.

Auburn, 516 4th NE, 939-8825
Bellevue, 601 143rd NE, 296-4262
Enumclaw, 420 Semanski S, 825-1188
Evergreen (Burien), 606 SW 116th, 296-4410
Federal Way, 30421 16th S, 839-1000

Issaquah, 50th & SE Clark, 296-4263
Kent, 25401 104th SE, 296-4275
King County Aquatics Center (Weyerhauser), 650 SW Campus Dr, Federal Way, 296-4444
Mercer Island, 8815 SE 40th, 296-4370
Mount Rainier, 22722 19th S, Des Moines, 296-4278
Northshore, 9815 NE 188th, Bothell, 296-4333
Redmond, 17535 NE 104th, 296-2961
Renton (Lindberg), 16740 128th SE, 296-4335
Saint Edwards State Park, 14445 Juanita Drive NE, Bothell, 296-2970
Shoreline, 19030 1st NE, Seattle, 296-4345
Si View, 41600 SE 122nd, North Bend, 889-1447
South Central (Foster), 4414 S144th, Seattle, 296-4487
Tahoma, 18230 SE 240th, Kent, 296-4276

(Vashon Island Pool is an outdoor pool open during the summer only. It is located at 9600 SW 204th, Vashon Island, 463-3787.)

Aqua Barn Ranch

15227 SE Renton-Maple Hwy in Renton
255-4618

Aqua Barn Ranch is a private facility with horseback riding and a large pool that is well-equipped with a slide, diving board and a good-sized kiddie pool. Kids can ride and swim all on the same day. Cost of admission is $2.43 for ages 12 and under; $2.93 for ages 14-18; $3.52 for adults. (See Active Play: Indoor Fun/Horseback Riding.)

CHAPTER 6

Spectator Sports

For many parents, the shared thrill of an exciting sports event is one of the first opportunities for common ground with their child. Although it is easy to get cynical about the corrupting influence of money and politics on professional sports, lessons in fair play, team cooperation, the agony of losing and the glory of winning still abound at all levels of team sports.

The cost of a family outing to a professional sporting event can be prohibitive, especially when you add parking and snack expenses to the cost of the tickets. Keep in mind that the professional teams don't necessarily provide the best entertainment. Don't forget to think of smaller arenas—such as local high schools and colleges— when hankering for a sports night out. You'll spend less, often see better games and better sports role models (male and female), and avoid the traffic hassles of the larger events.

The following listings include both professional and lower division spectator sports in the Seattle area. When you call for tickets, ask about good seating areas in your price range and discounts for kids.

The Big Guys

Seattle Mariners

Games at the Kingdome
628-3555; Ticketmaster, 628-0888
Season runs April-September
$5.50-$12.50; prices for kids, $4-$5

In 1992, the Seattle Mariners Baseball Club just about left Seattle to become the Tampa/St. Petersburg, Florida, team. It was a strange and twisted situation that caused national schisms for baseball, bringing up such questions as "Can a non-American own a baseball team?" (Yes, as long as he is not the primary owner) and "Can a politician save face by saving baseball?" (Guess so, because US Senator Slade Gorton pulled some political magic for the M's, making himself look pretty goll-dern all-American). As it turns out, the Mariners are still in the Emerald City, with a surprisingly dedicated following despite the team's overall lackluster performance.

In its favor, the Seattle Mariner Baseball Club has made a special effort to make America's pastime affordable and fun for families. Many special promotional events are offered throughout the season, featuring a variety of souvenir giveaways and incentives like free bats, t-shirts or caps for the first several thousand kids in the Kingdome. Several games are designated as Family Nights, offering half-price tickets for adults.

To keep the game interesting during those inevitable slow points when the Charlie Browns of the team are at bat, the Kingdome's giant replay screen flashes mini-hydro races, magic tricks, trivia and much more—designed to keep everyone in the family entertained. And if the M's hit a homerun, you'll get a quick change of scenery: a fireworks display. Most younger kids will actually sit through all nine innings in anticipation of this event (just hope it happens).

> ☆ ***Tips***
> *If you want a little different perspective on a Mariner game, get seats overlooking third base. You'll get a surprisingly good view of the game, plus an interesting sideshow, because the pitchers warm up on this side of the field.*

☆ *Essentials*

Food at the Kingdome is no bargain, but the hot dogs are yummy and the foil bags of hot peanuts, nostalgic. If you want to save money, you are allowed to bring in your own food, though beverages are prohibited.

Seattle Seahawks
Games at the Kingdome
Ticket office, 827-9766
Season runs August-December
$19-$35

Despite several dismal seasons, the Seattle Seahawks enjoy a loyal following of tens of thousands of season ticket holders. Only about 2,000 tickets are available to the general public for any single game, and no ticket price discounts are offered. Parents have varying opinions about whether taking in a Seahawks game is a good family activity. We'd recommend that you only take the kids who are into football and old enough to understand the complexity of the sport.

Seattle SuperSonics
Games at the Coliseum, Seattle Center (some at the Kingdome)
281-5800; ticket office, 281-5850
Season runs September-May
$7-$42

Though they've definitely experienced some bad seasons, the SuperSonics are presently a hot team. It does gets pricey to take kids to a Sonics game and the parking situation is not so hot, but if you have the money and patience to spare, do so: Your school-age child will probably become a real fan of both basketball and you (at least for the duration of the game).

Aside from inducing a noisy, spirited atmosphere, the

Seahawks games are an expensive but exciting outing for young football fans.

SuperSonics do a good job of providing diversions with their Sasquatch mascot, entertainment at timeouts, a toy blimp that cruises around inside the Coliseum dropping prizes, and other treats. During the regular season, special day-of-game discounts are available after 5 pm for children 14 and under at the Seattle Center Coliseum. Call 281-5850 for details.

☆ *Essentials*

You can bring your own food into the Coliseum (not beverages). Otherwise plan on eating the regular fare of hot dogs, pretzels and popcorn at the usual high prices.

Seattle Thunderbirds

Games at the Seattle Center Arena and Coliseum
Ticket office, 365 Mercer St
Seattle
448-PUCK
Season runs September-March
$7-$10

Since Old Man Winter doesn't freeze the ponds around here very often, it's easy to forget about hockey and other ice sports. But we do have a Western Hockey League team known as the Seattle Thunderbirds, and if you think your child would enjoy the fast-paced action, it's a fun and easily comprehensible sport to watch.

The downside of hockey is usually the raucous atmosphere and obnoxious crowd. (Some people claim to go to games solely for the colorful fights that take place in the rink.) If you can tolerate those negatives, the Thunderbirds promise some competitive, exciting entertainment. The Thunderbirds offer $1-off tickets for kids under 14 throughout their regular season.

The Little Guys

Everett Giants

Everett Memorial Stadium, 39th & Broadway, Everett; just off of I-5
258-3673; Ticketmaster, 628-0888
Season runs June-September
$3.50-$6.50

Recapture the romance of baseball on green grass under the open sky on a warm summer night. Sing "Take Me Out to the Ball Game" and mean it. At these games you'll find decent prices, good entertainment for those inevitiable slow stretches (like real fireworks), tasty hot dogs and some fine ball handling. The Everett Giants, a Class A Affiliate of the San Francisco Giants, play baseball from June to September at their home field, Everett Memorial Stadium. The stadium complex includes a children's play field with wide open spaces to throw a ball, run and chase foul balls.

☆ *Essentials*

Go to the game hungry, because you can fill up on surprisingly good food for roughly $5 a person. Aside from the regular fare, the Everett Memorial Stadium offers raw vegetable plates, barbecued items and much more. Be sure to save room for the delectable "Chocolate Thunder" cake, available at the coffee and dessert stand.

Tacoma Tigers

Cheney Stadium, Tacoma, just off I-5
752-7707
Season runs April-September
$3.50-$4.50; discounts for children, seniors & military personnel

The Tacoma Tigers are an Oakland Athletics Class AAA Affiliate, just one step away from major league baseball! Games are played outdoors at Cheney Stadium in Tacoma. The season features several promotional activities, including souvenir giveaways, family tailgate parties and a special fireworks show every Fourth of July.

University of Washington Huskies

543-2200

At UW sporting events you will find highly talented athletes and great competition at a fraction of the cost of the professional games. UW Women's Basketball (November-March) is at the top of the Pac Ten and has recently become one of the most popular sporting events in town. The games are thrilling and exhibit the frequently overlooked talent of women in the sports world—important for both young girls and young boys to see. Tickets are reasonably priced at $5 and $7.

Husky Football (September-November) tickets range from $12 to $26 and usually sell out, not only because the team is outstanding, but because alumni are fervently dedicated and often reluctant to give up their season tickets before they die.

Other UW sports teams include

With the marching band and all the hoopla from the students, Husky games are fun for kids even if they don't understand football.

Photo credit: Joanie Komura

baseball (February-June), played outdoors on real grass ($4/adults; $2/children), and gymnastics (January-March), a fun winter diversion ($4/adults; $2 children).

Tickets are sold at the Ticket Office just north of HEC Edmundson Pavilion, adjacent to Husky Stadium. Call 543-2200 for schedule and ticket information.

Velodrome Bike Racing

Marymoor Park, Redmond
389-5825

One of only 19 velodromes in the United States, the velodrome at Marymoor Park in Redmond features a full season of bicycle racing and events. From mid-May until early September, on two evenings per week at 7:30 pm, the Velodrome features bicycle racing. Admission is free on Thursday nights when races are open to beginning racers and those people not interested in training for competitive racing. Kids can participate if they are at least five-feet tall, but the steep slopes of the track are often intimidating. Friday night is probably the best night to go as a spectator, because Olympic-style track racing is featured. On Friday, admission for spectators is $3.

> ☆ ***Tips***
>
> *Bring cushions to sit on—the bleachers at the Velodrome aren't exactly comfortable. Marymoor is a wonderful park, so if you or your children get restless, take advantage of the surrounding lawns and open spaces. (See Parks for more information on Marymoor.)*

CHAPTER 7

Kid Culture

Give your kids some culture? Yeah, right. It's hard enough to get them to take baths, let alone drag them into a museum. And at least with a bath, you can see results. Visiting the art world is a much more subtle cleansing—sort of a polishing of the senses.

The fact of the matter is that museum exhibits, theatre performances and musical concerts can be intimidating even for adults, and taking your kids to such events can be like taking them to a remote land where no one speaks your language. What you might not know is how many of our local arts organizations have programs designed especially for kids, to help them learn to appreciate art on their level.

"Each second we live is a new and unique moment of the universe, a moment that never was before and never will be again. And what do we teach our children in school? We teach them two and two make four and that Paris is the capital of France. When will we also teach them what they are? We should say to each of them: Do you know what you are? You are a marvel. You are unique. In all of the world there is no other child exactly like you. In the millions of years that have passed, there never has been a child like you. And look at your body — what a wonder it is! Your legs, your arms, your cunning fingers, the way you move! You may become a Shakespeare, a Michelangelo, a Beethoven. You have the capacity for anything. Yes, you are a marvel. And when you grow up, can you then harm another who is, like you, a marvel? You must cherish one another. You must work — we must all work — to make this world worthy of its children."

-Pablo Casals

Exhibits & Museums

Bellevue Art Museum

301 Bellevue Way NE, Bellevue; Third Floor, Bellevue Square
454-6021
Mon-Sat, 10 am-6 pm; open Tues & Fri until 8 pm; Sun, 11 am-5 pm
$3/adults; $2/seniors & students; children 12 & under free. Museum admission is free on Tuesday
Annual membership: $40/family

It's natural to be skeptical about having a cultural experience in a shopping mall, but don't let that stop you from visiting the Bellevue Art Museum on the third floor of Bellevue Square. BAM is accessible by elevator or stairs from the main retail shop area and is easily negotiated by strollers. The museum, which has no permanent collection, showcases five or six different exhibits each year and is small and intimate—a good size that won't overwhelm kids.

If you have kids of varied ages, it's likely that the older ones will find culture in the mall itself, so let them run off while you and the younger kids become enlightened.

☆ Essentials

There are several good spots to eat lunch or grab a quick snack within the mall, some favorites being McDonald's, Pizza Haven, the Muffin Break, Steamers (fish and chips), and Jungle Jim's (a fun hamburger joint where kids under 12 eat for free).

Nearby Attractions: Bellevue Downtown Park, Bellefield Nature Park, Kelsey Creek Farm, Rosalie Whyel Doll Museum.

☆ Tips

Each year (usually during the months of November and December), the Bellevue Art Museum features a special exhibit designed specifically for children and families as part of its Celebration Especially for Children series. During this exhibit, workshops and classes for children are offered to complement the artwork on display. Volunteer docents host free tours of the featured exhibit every day at 2 pm, or you can prearrange a private tour. Both options are open to all ages. The museum's Gallery Shop, which is open during Bellevue Square's hours, has a special section especially for kids.

The Boat play area on the first floor of Bellevue Square is a good place for young kids to release some extra energy after visiting BAM.

Thomas Burke Memorial Washington State Museum

17th Ave NE & NE 45th St, Seattle;
University of Washington
543-5590
Open daily, 10 am-5 pm; Thursday evenings until 8 pm
Admission is by suggested donation: $3/adults; $2/seniors & students; $1.50/ages 6-18 years; children ages 5 & under free
Annual membership: $35/family

Just ask your kids if they'd like to see an authentic dinosaur skeleton, and (unless they were traumatized by "Jurassic Park"), you're as good as on your way to the Thomas Burke Memorial Washington State Museum, located on the north end of the University of Washington campus. The Burke Museum is the state museum of natural history and anthropology, featuring the only dinosaur skeleton on display in the Northwest; a collection of canoes, paddles and canoe-making tools of the Native Northwest peoples; artifacts from throughout the Pacific Rim; and a user-friendly touch-screen computer, which allows visitors to view the extensive Northwest Native art collection. The Discovery Room provides an opportunity for children to explore natural history through various hands-on activities, which change to complement special exhibits. The museum store is chock full of special items for kids including books, puppets, dinosaurs, toys and games.

☆ Essentials

Trying to find a parking space on campus on a weekday while school is in session can be difficult, but there are several public lots to choose from along University Way and near campus. Carpools of three or more persons can park on campus for $2, and anyone can park for free after 12 pm on Saturday and all day Sunday. Metro (553-3000) also has several buses that stop near campus.

If you want to revive your group with a snack, the museum cafe offers a delicious selection of "coffee shop" goodies, such as scones, cookies, muffins and lattes, as well as a few sandwich selections. If it's a nice day, take the time after your museum visit to stroll through the campus. Red Square is a bricked expanse that offers running space (when student traffic is low), beautiful architecture and a spectacular view of Mount Rainier and the campus' Drumheller Fountain. The Graduate Library, Suzzalo, is the architectural highlight of campus, and if your kids are well-behaved (or have laryngitis), it deserves a quick tour. Up from this square to the northeast, is the grassy Quad, which is stunning in the early spring when the trees are blossoming. If you had an aerial view, you would see that the trees are planted in the shape of a "W."

Nearby attractions: Henry Art Gallery, University Book Store, UW Observatory, UW Waterfront Activity Center.

> ☆ ***Tips***
>
> *If your children are nocturnal, or just ask lots of questions about the night sky, go back to the UW campus at night to visit the UW Observatory. Located at 17th Ave NE & 45th (across from the Burke Museum), the Observatory is open to the public Monday, Wednesday and Thursday, 9-11 pm (open during UW school breaks, except major holidays).*
>
> *On clear nights, visitors can look at the sky through a 6-inch refractor telescope; on cloudy nights, a slide show on astronomy is presented. Guides are on site to answer questions and help with the operation of the telescope.*
>
> *Admission is free; all ages are welcome. Children should be accompanied by an adult. (Large groups need to make reservations by calling 543-2888).*
>
> *Call 543-0126 for more details.*

The Center for Wooden Boats
1010 Valley St, Seattle
382-2628
Open year-round, Wed-Mon, 12-6 pm; closed Tuesday
Free admission; donations gladly accepted
Annual membership: $40/family

It is difficult to be a resident of the 'Boating Capital of the World' without catching at least a little boating fever. The Center for Wooden Boats at the south end of Lake Union is a great place to show your kids some of the most beautiful boats ever built. This floating museum and shop features a collection of approximately 60 wooden boats, many of them moored along the docks, ranging from the smallest dinghy to a three-masted schooner. Stroll along the docks (parents can stop by the Oar House or Boat House and borrow life vests for the little ones) and enjoy the floating collection. Children can climb aboard the Panesano, a Monterey fishing boat, work the wheel and imagine they're the captain of their own ship!

The staff at the center builds and restores water craft of all sizes using a variety of tools from the past and the present, so there is always some boat-building or restoring activity going on in the shop. You might even get an impromptu lesson on varnishing, rope tying or woodworking during your visit.

Inside the Boat House you'll find old photos, canoes and shells hanging from the ceiling, and an old binnacle (a housing for the large compass on a big ship), which children can explore. The Boat House also features several models of boats, as well as a library that contains a collection of children's books.

☆ Tips

During the summer months, skiffs, canoes, sailboats and kayaks are available for hourly rental from the Boat House. The cost to rent rowing and paddling crafts is $8-$12 per hour; rentals for sailing craft start at $10 per hour. Life jackets are supplied for everyone. Call 382-BOAT for information.

If you are in town over the Fourth of July weekend, the annual Wooden Boat Festival is a fun diversion. Activities include small boat races, music, food, contests and working exhibits. Kids can participate in special programs designed to teach maritime skills. Admission is free.

The Center for Wooden Boats also offers family sailing lessons.

☆ Essentials

Parking is free. Quite a few good restaurants are within walking distance of the center, including Burger King and Cucina!Cucina! a good, inexpensive Italian spot, which has an excellent kid's menu. During the summer months, try Benji's—a small outdoor fish and chips stand shaped like a tugboat, which is located just outside Benjamin's on the lake. Benji's fish and chips are delicious, as is the coleslaw.

Nearby attractions: Gas Works Park, Northwest Outdoor Center.

Photo credit: Children's Museum

In the Children's Museum's child-sized neighborhood, kids act out adult roles.

Children's Museum

Seattle Center House, Lower Level
441-1768
Tues-Sun, 10 am-5 pm; open daily during the summer months
$3.50/person; children under 12 months are free
Annual membership: $35/family

Remember how much fun it was when you were a kid and the whole world was make-believe? You could do anything and go anywhere in your imagination. The Children's Museum offers the best in creative, interactive play for young children today. The crux of this museum is a child-sized neighborhood, where kids can move from establishment to establishment and role play. It includes a supermarket for grocery shopping, a Metro bus to drive, a doctor's office equipped with instruments to check vital signs, a theater where kids can create their own screenplays and much more. The fun is creative, imaginative and educational.

Admission to the museum also includes daily hands-on workshops, in which children create their own special crafts, as well as entry to Imagination Station, the museum's drop-in art studio, where kids can work with professional artists to

☆ *Tips*

The Children's Museum is a good outing for an active toddler. The special toddler play area features a foam playground with an under-the-sea motif. Kids under two and a half can climb all over a padded whale and safely burn off excess energy. If you need to bring along an older child, who might be bored by most of the exhibits, steer them to the Legos room, where they will find mounds of Legos to keep them occupied. The Children's Museum also has an excellent gift shop filled with quality educational toys.

Just to the north of the museum is a candy shop where kids can watch salt water taffy being made.

create a variety of art masterpieces. Both the hands-on workshops and activities at Imagination Station are excellent, featuring quick and interesting creative activities the kids can really sink their hands into.

The Children's Museum is due for expansion in 1994; it will be tripled in size.

☆ *Essentials*

Food choices are abundant in the Center House Food Circus, just up the stairs from The Children's Museum. Recommendations include Baker's yummy frozen chocolate-covered bananas, Cafe Loc's Vietnamese noodles and The Frankfurter's hot dogs.

Nearby attractions: Located within the Seattle Center Grounds are the Pacific Science Center, the Space Needle, the Coliseum, the Pacific Arts Center, the Fun Forest, the Food Circus and ample room to picnic and roam. A short Monorail ride from the Seattle Center takes you to the retail district of downtown Seattle including Westlake Mall. From there, a walk of a few blocks takes you to Pike Place Market.

Henry Art Gallery

15th Ave NE & NE 41st St, Seattle; University of Washington
543-2280
Tues-Sun, 10 am-5 pm; Thursday evenings until 9 pm
$3/adults; $1.50/students & seniors; children under 13 free; admission is free every Thursday
Annual membership: $40/family

The Henry opens new exhibits about every six to twelve weeks, showcasing a variety of artists and artistic mediums. It has one of the most successful and well-designed educational programs in the city, offering lectures, workshops, classes and tours. The children's workshops, led by professional artists, bring even the most esoteric of exhibits within reach of kids' creativity and understanding, and are highly participatory. (Be sure to preregister your child for any workshops or events—they are quite popular.)

Courtesy of the Henry Gallery, photo credit: Richard Nicol.

Detail from A Sansei Story, by Roger Shimomura. Acrylic on canvas, 1990.

The Henry was the first public art museum in Washington state, donated to the people of Washington in 1927 by Horace C. Henry, a local tycoon. Included in this donation was his personal collection of early 20th century works. The state legislature recently approved expansion plans for the museum (projected for completion in mid-1996), which will create the necessary space to mount exhibits from its permanent collection of approximately 18,000 works.

☆ *Essentials*

See Burke Museum.

Nearby attractions: Arboretum, Burke Museum, Museum of History and Industry, University Book Store, UW Waterfront Activity Center.

The Art Student. Acrylic, sumi, collage by Faye Jones,1990. Courtesy of the Microsoft Art Collection, photo credit: Richard Nicol.

☆ *Tips*

On designated Saturday afternoons during each exhibition at the Henry Art Gallery, free docent-led tours are scheduled for families with children five years and older. Special age-appropriate docent-led school and group tours are also offered with each exhibition. These pre-arranged group tours are presented free of charge. Teachers and parents are encouraged to contact the Curator of Education to receive information on tours and curriculum guides.

Klondike Gold Rush National Historical Park

117 S Main, Seattle
553-7220
Open daily, 9 am-5 pm
Free admission

Maybe, on the surface, the gold rush of the 1800s is about as interesting for you as a red-tag sale at K-Mart. So, maybe you and your kids have passed by this little museum in Pioneer Square dozens of times. But think about it this way: Everyone can relate to wanting to strike it rich, and because of this age-old desire, Seattle was able to prosper in its early years. Why not go inside and get the scoop? This museum actually tells a pretty good story, which makes it fun for all ages.

National Park Service, which set up this historical park, has done a thorough job in using a variety of media, including maps, photos, slides and films, to document the Gold Rush and its enormous effect on the City of Seattle. Your kids will enjoy seeing the shovels, picks and other tools used by the prospectors, and watching the rangers demonstrate how they panned for gold. A visit through this interesting park is a quick and easy stop, and once you do it, you and your kids will know at least two things: Learning history can be painless and finding gold is easier dreamt than done.

☆ ***Tips***
Ask for the Kids Activity Booklet at the Information Desk in the Klondike Historical Park—it will encourage the children to explore the museum and their own neighborhoods.

☆ ***Essentials***

See Exploring Downtown/ Pioneer Square.

Nearby attractions: Pioneer Square including retail shops, cafes and galleries, the Kingdome and the Seattle Waterfront. Catch the Waterfront Streetcar for a scenic ride along the Waterfront to Pier 70.

Museum of Flight
9404 E Marginal Way S, Seattle; located at Boeing Field
764-5700
Open daily, 10 am-5 pm; Thursday evenings until 9 pm
$5/adults; $3/children ages 6-15; children under 6 free; free parking
Annual membership: $35/family

Who in your family gets excited about a trip to the airport, even if they are not going anywhere? The prevalence of knee-high handprints on airport windows gives it away. Most kids are completely in awe of the steel birds that grace the sky, which is why the Museum of Flight is a popular destination for families. This wonderful museum explores the history of flight from the earliest aircraft to the space stations of the future.

Located within the museum's vast, open Great Gallery is the hangar exhibit, which features three aircraft (biplane, monoplane and helicopter), a variety of tools, spare aircraft parts, engines, workbenches and helmets. Young aircraft enthusiasts will enjoy this place

☆ *Tips*

A new exhibit at the Museum of Flight, the Challenger Learning Center, features mock-ups of a 21st-century Space Station and a Mission Control facility, with plenty of hands-on activities designed for students in grades five to nine. These Learning Center school programs include two hours of teamwork, in which students work to solve mathematics, science and technology problems. Mini-Missions, a shorter version of these workshops, are offered to the general public during designated hours on specific days, presenting an opportunity to work the equipment in the Space Station during a 30-minute simulated hop into outer space. (Children under 10 must be accompanied by an adult.) The center is the only one of its kind in the Northwest.

Special events are held throughout the year at the Museum of Flight, including the annual family-focused Flight Festival held in July. This event features visiting aircraft, aerobatic performances, hands-on educational programs, live music and entertainment. Special drop-in programs are held throughout the year in The Hangar as well, which teach young people about the skills needed to design, build and maintain aircraft. Family hands-on workshops are held throughout the year, offering an opportunity for youngsters to design gliders, learn about hot-air balloons and much more. Most of these workshops are appropriate for children ages five and up and their parents.

immensely—the aircraft are full-scale, and there is plenty of room to move about.

Any Navy Blue Angels fans will appreciate the full-scale mock-up of the Northrop F/A 18 at the museum. This jet fighter measures 56 feet in length with a wing span of 40.5 feet, and features a moveable joystick, control panels and radar screens. Children can climb into the cockpit and pretend they are part of the flight aerobatic team!

☆ *Essentials*

Metro Bus Route 174 takes you right to the museum from Sea-Tac or downtown Seattle. If driving, take Exit 158 from I-5 and follow the signs along E Marginal Way for about 1/4 of a mile. Parking is abundant and free. Strollers are not available for rent, although you can easily negotiate one throughout the exhibit. The museum currently offers an espresso cart fully equipped with soda, hot dogs and such; a new cafe will open in the spring of 1994.

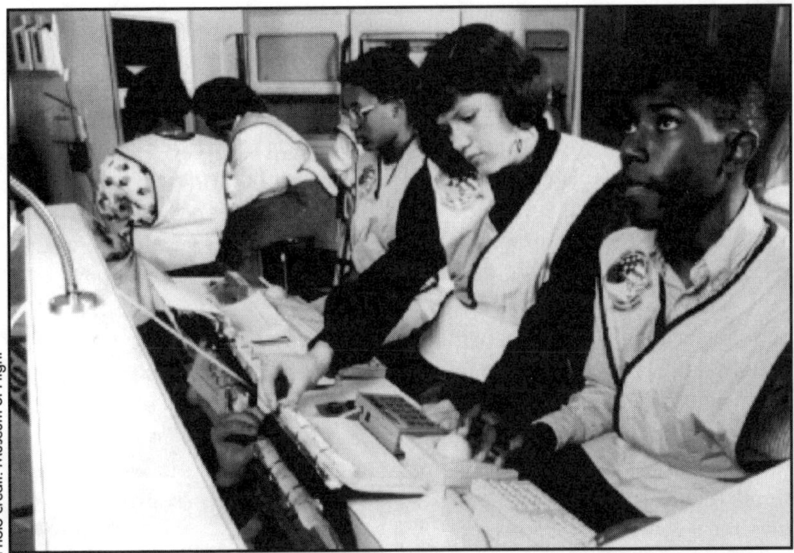

Photo credit: Museum of Flight

Students in the Challenger Learning Center apply math, science and technology to successfully complete a simulated mission into outer space.

Museum of History & Industry

2700 24th Ave E, Seattle; just south of Husky Stadium
324-1126
Open daily, 10 am-5 pm
$3/adults, $1.50/children ages 6-12; free parking
Annual membership: $35/family

The Museum of History and Industry continues to do an outstanding job of designing new exhibits and programs that encourage the entire family to experience Seattle and Northwest history. Permanent exhibits include the Seattle Fire exhibit, which educates children about the fire that ravaged the city in 1889 and shows some of the antiquated equipment used to battle the flames; the Seattle Story, a historical timeline of Seattle from 1850 to the present; and the 1880s Gallery, a full-scale model of a section of First Ave, featuring a barber shop, a general store and other shops.

Another popular permanent attraction is an authentic B-1 airplane that hangs from the ceiling. It was the first commercial aircraft built by Boeing in the early 1900s, designed to run air mail service over international lines.

Hands-On History is another permanent exhibit, with changing themes. Here, kids participate in many activities, ranging from trying on the clothes of past eras to loading a model container ship with wooden blocks. In addition, the museum offers special events for families throughout the year, designed to complement and enhance the temporary exhibits.

The Gift Shop at the entrance to the museum has many interesting items for sale including copies of old Seattle newspapers — for example, the edition of the paper that came out the day after the collapse of the Tacoma Narrows bridge.

☆ *Essentials*

The layout of this museum is open and spacious. There is ample room to maneuver wheelchairs and strollers, and free parking is available on the grounds. No food is available in the immediate area, but you can bring a snack to enjoy outside the museum while the kids climb on the giant cannon that sits next to the lower parking lot.

Nearby attractions: Arboretum, Henry Art Gallery, University Book Store, UW Waterfront Activity Center.

☆ *Tips*

The Museum of History and Industry is a good place to visit with kids because the exhibits will truly hold their attention. The staff is friendly and helpful and welcomes young visitors.

Adjacent to the museum's parking lot is a waterfront pathway that leads to nearby Foster Island. This is a great walk for kids; they enjoy negotiating the little bridges along the way and watching the boat action at the Montlake cut.

Nordic Heritage Museum

3014 NW 67th St, Seattle; located in Ballard
789-5707
Tues-Sat, 10 am-4 pm; Sun, 12-4 pm
$3/general; $2/seniors & college students; $1/grades K-12; admission is free on the first Tuesday of every month
Annual membership: $30/family

The Nordic Heritage Museum in Ballard is the only museum in North America showcasing the cultures of the five major Scandinavian countries: Denmark, Finland, Iceland, Norway and Sweden. The museum educates children and their families about the essential contributions made by these immigrants, many of whom settled in Seattle's Ballard neighborhood. The museum also offers a variety of educational programs, from traveling trunks, curriculum materials and speakers to teacher workshops, and a variety of special events for all ages. Future plans for the museum include space for a children's gallery.

☆ *Essentials*

The museum is located in a renovated school, with plenty of free parking. If you get in the spirit of things, Scandies on Market St in downtown Ballard offers tasty and authentic Scandinavian food, but it's a good 12-block walk to downtown Ballard from the museum. Another good food spot (near the Hiram M. Chittenden Locks) is the Totem House, which serves some of the best fish and chips in town.

Nearby attractions: Golden Gardens, Hiram M. Chittenden Government Locks.

☆ *Tips*

The Nordic Heritage Museum hosts annual special events for families, including Ballard's Nordic Yulefest, a Nordic pre-Christmas holiday event held in November, and Tivoli—A Bite of Scandinavia, a Scandinavian summer festival held in July. All events include music, food and children's activities.

Circle of Friends, a special event featuring games, storytelling, native foods, costumes, crafts and songs, is held six times each year at the museum. It is designed to allow children to celebrate and explore cultures of various countries.

Pacific Arts Center

305 Harrison, Seattle; located at the Seattle Center
443-5437
Tues-Sat, 10 am-4 pm
Nominal admission; donations appreciated
Annual membership: $25/family

Pacific Arts Center began as a volunteer program in the 1940s, bringing storytelling and arts experiences to children in the Seattle area. In the early '80s the organization moved into the old Nile Temple at the Seattle Center and became a non-profit educational center, offering monthly exhibits and programs for children and adults. At press time, it was under renovation.

The refurbished Pacific Arts Center will open in August 1993, with a full array of classes and workshops in all artistic disciplines. This new facility will include more gallery space, as well as three classrooms, a gift shop and a resource library. Exhibits will still be created with children in mind, and often feature works created by young people in town. Aurora Valentinetti's (former University of Washington professor) puppets will be part of the Center's permanent collection.

Pacific Arts Center will also continue its extensive ArtsReach program, which serves at-risk and homeless children throughout the

Photo credit: Pacific Science Center

The Bubble Festival at The Pacfic Science Center is a fabulous place for kids to learn about science while they play.

area, as well as a full-arts curriculum after-school program for elementary and junior high students.

☆ *Essentials*

See Exploring Downtown/Seattle Center.

☆ *Tips*

Though you can drop in for classes and workshops at the Pacific Arts Center, preregistration is recommended because space is limited.

Pacific Science Center

200 Second Ave N, Seattle; located at the Seattle Center
443-2001
Mon-Fri, 10 am-5 pm; Sat, Sun and holidays, 10 am-6 pm
$6.50/adults; $5.50/children 6-13 years & seniors; $4.50/children 2-5 years
Annual membership: $35/family

The Pacific Science Center is a nationally renowned organization filled with exhibits that reinforce a positive attitude toward science, making it fun, experimental and participatory. Kids can go from exhibit to exhibit, testing their eyesight, weight, strength and eating habits; experimenting with different musical instruments, bubbles, mirrors and gravity; finding out by doing not just watching.

One of the larger theme exhibits explores the era of dinosaurs and features five moving, roaring, robotic dinosaurs. (Many preschoolers choose to stand outside the door to this exhibit and just peak inside.) Kids can stand in a gigantic footprint of a duckbill dinosaur or operate the controls of a dinosaur model.

Another section of the Pacific Science Center, the Kids Works area, features a playground for young kids called "Just for Tots" (persons over 48 inches tall can't get in unless accompanying a tot). Another popular activity within the Kids Works is the KKID News studio, where kids can film each other doing a news broadcast.

After all the energetic exploration, the IMAX Theatre, in the

> ☆ ***Tips***
>
> *The Pacific Science Center is one of those rare places that everyone in the family will enjoy (you may be surprised how many teenagers are there having a good time). There is no certain order in which you should see the exhibits. Think of it as a science playground and allow plenty of time.*
>
> *Popular annual events not to miss are the Model Railroad Show in November, the Science Circus, held during the holiday break between Christmas and New Year's, and the Bubble Festival, held each August.*
>
> *The gift shop is outstanding—one of the best places in town to find creative, educational toys and children's books. Save time for browsing.*
>
> *Teachers and others concerned with providing science and mathematics education may be interested in purchasing the Pacific Science Center's Explore More Store Resource Guide. It is a valuable 250-page catalog of over 1700 products that help kids learn about science and math, including books, posters, activity kits, games and toys. Catalog cost is $5; call 443-2870 to order.*

upper west corner of the Science Center, is an excellent place to relax and have a truly unforgettable movie experience. The outstanding IMAX movies are shot on 70-mm film and shown on a screen three and a half stories high. Tickets may pe purchased as you enter the Science Center, or you can just go to IMAX. Cost is $4.50/adults; $3.50/children 6-13 years; $3.50/seniors; $2.50/children under 5. (One free movie is included with admission to the Science Center.) Watch out—popular movies fill up early on busy days.

Laser Fantasy is another theatre inside the Science Center that is well worth experiencing. (It is also one of the few places in town that provides good evening entertainment for teen-age kids.) Viewers lie back in comfy chairs or stretch out on the carpeted floor to watch a lazer light show accompanied by music. Evening shows feature music popular with teens—Laser Zepplin, Laser U-2, Guns and Roses, etc. The matinee show is a space odessey set to classical and popular music and provides a soothing break. Cost is $3/show or $6 for all three evening shows. (One free show is included with admission to the Science Center). Call the Laser Hot Line at 443-2850 for schedule information.

☆ Essentials

All exhibits at the center are stroller and wheelchair accessible. A stroller is recommended rather than a backpack so you can easily let loose a curious child who wants to explore. (The Science Center is meant to be a completely hands-on experience for your child, so you might want to skip carrying equipment altogether.) A changing table is located in the women's restroom in Building 6; Building 3 is currently being renovated and will also have a changing table when completed (November '93). The food at the cafe is good, offering a selection of made-to-order deli sandwiches, soups and salads, as well as the usual snacks including cookies, coffee and juices.

Nearby attractions: See In & Around Downtown/Seattle Center

Rosalie Whyel Museum of Doll Art

1116 108th Ave NE, Bellevue
455-1116
Mon-Sat, 10 am-5 pm; Thursday evenings until 8 pm; Sun, 1-5 pm
$5/adults; $4.50/seniors; $4/children 5-17 years; children under 5 free
Annual pass: $50/family

What's big and pink and full of dolls? Believe it or not, the Rosalie Whyel Museum of Doll Art. This 13,000-square-foot, baby-pink Victorian-style mansion is home to 1,050 dolls—Whyel's collection. The museum, which cost her $3.5 million to build, opened in the fall of 1992 to exhibit the history, technology and artistry of doll making. Whyel's collection appeals to all ages, from preschool to seniors, and includes everything from antique dolls dating back to the year 1650 to Barbie, as well as toys, teddy bears and other childhood memorabilia. The collection even includes two Egyptian tomb dolls dating back to sometime B.C. All the displays are housed within glass cases, safe from little hands.

The museum holds assembly presentations at elementary and secondary schools, which educate children about the artistry and history of doll making.

Nearby attractions: Bellevue Art Museum, Bellevue Square, Meydenbauer Park.

Seattle Art Museum

100 University St, downtown Seattle
654-3100
Tues-Sun, 10 am-5 pm; Thurs, 10 am-9 pm; open select Mon holidays
$6/adults; $4/seniors, disabled persons & students; children 12 and under are admitted free when accompanied by an adult; admission is free the first Tuesday of each month
Annual membership: $50/family

It's always a blessing when Seattle voters loosen their wallets to fund something cultural, especially when it's for something as critical to a city's heartbeat as a museum. Thanks to their support, the Seattle Art Museum has a beautiful new

Photo credit: Susan Dirk

Hammering Man at the southwest entrance to the downtown Seattle Art Museum.

"I would hope that children who see the Hammering Man at work would connect their delight with the potential mysteries that a museum could offer them in their future."

—Jonathan Borofsky, Hammering Man artist

Photo credit: Susan Dirk

Chinese Qing-Dynasty marble tomb guardian figures from an unknown Manchu tomb near Bejing stand on the grand stairway inside the Seattle Art Museum.

home and a marvelous education program that truly encourages children and families to experience art on a level comfortable to them. The museum has been applauded for making the art world less stifling and intimidating for everyone.

The Seattle Art Museum has had some diehard fans through the years, perhaps most notably its founder and primary benefactor, Dr. Richard E. Fuller. His collections of Japanese and Chinese art and other works formed a small but important holding for the Seattle Art Museum, which he and his family financed and opened in 1933 in Volunteer Park. Fuller retired in 1973 and died in '76.

SAM opened its downtown location in late 1991, under the directorship of Jay Gates. The kids will recognize the Seattle Art Museum by the famous 48-foot tall *Hammering Man*, weighing in at over 20,000 pounds, located just outside the building. The museum's design, by Robert Venturi, is spacious and bright, and the collection, which has grown to include early European works, African art, modern art and photography as well as Asian works, is exquisitely exhibited.

Of special interest to children is the collection of ancient jade carvings on the third floor. Try to pick out the rooster, lions, camels and other figures within these intricate carvings! The fourth floor, which houses the modern art collection, is always fun to explore with kids, mostly just to watch their reactions to the abstract pieces (but don't take any child who is in that stage of asking "Why?" every five seconds).

On the first floor, visitors will find the user-friendly interactive touch-screen computer, View Point, which offers loads of information and a close-up look at the artwork housed within the museum. Special exhibitions are presented several times per year, showcasing traveling exhibits or special selections from the museum's permanent collection.

☆ *Essentials*

Several public parking garages and lots are located within walking distance of the museum including one adjacent to SAM (prices vary), however several Metro bus routes stop right outside the museum, so that may be more convenient (call 553-3000 for information on how to get to SAM from anywhere in King County). SAM is fully accessible to strollers and wheelchairs. Wheelchairs are available for use while in the museum; strollers are not available for rent.

There is a good cafe in the museum, off the main stairwell. If it's too crowded, walk a couple blocks to the Pike Place Market (1st Ave and Pike St), and grab a snack at any one of the many restaurants there. (See In & Around Downtown/Pike Place Market for a detailed look at this area.)

Nearby attractions: Pike Place Market, a free ride aboard a Metro bus takes you to Pioneer Square and the Waterfront.

Wing Luke Asian Museum

407 7th Ave S, Seattle
623-5124
Tues-Fri, 11 am-4:30 pm; Sat-Sun, 12-4 pm
$2.50/adults; $1.50/seniors & students; $.75/children 5-12 years
Annual membership: $50/family

The Wing Luke Asian Museum, located in Seattle's historic International District, showcases the many contributions of Seattle's Asian communities. Seattle's international population comprises many Asian cultures, and the Wing Luke Museum is devoted to illustrating the great diversity among them. The museum recently opened a new permanent exhibit entitled One Song, Many Voices, which tells the 200-year story of immigration and settlement of Asians and Pacific Islanders in Washington state. Visitors will see 85 photos and over 200 artifacts—many of which were donated by individuals from different communities—illustrating immigration, employment, community life, discrimination and cultural traditions. The museum welcomes about 30,000 children each year from schools and other community groups around the area and offers tours and craft sessions to complement the featured exhibits.

☆ *Essentials*

One of Metro's underground stations is located in the heart of the International District at 5th and Jackson, where you can catch buses to Pioneer Square, University Street, Westlake Mall and Convention Place, free of charge. See In & Around Downtown/International District.

Nearby attractions: Pioneer Square, Seattle Waterfront.

Radio

KidStar

1250 AM
382-1250

As of mid-May 1993, Puget Sound area kids have a radio station they can call their own. KidStar AM 1250 is a hip alternative to television, featuring "diverse, professionally produced, high-quality entertainment, delivered in an intelligent and respectful way." Programming includes all the elements of "adult" radio—music, weather, news, and stories—but in a way that speaks to kids in their pre-teen years.

A big component of the KidStar network is an interactive phone system called the PhoneZone, which allows kids to call (for free) to participate in contests and opinion polls and to access a variety of different extensions (laugh line, question of the week, etc.). Before a child can call up PhoneZone, however, she must obtain a secret code by becoming a KidStar All-Star (a free membership).

KidStar has been endorsed by the Washington State Parent Teachers Association and judging by the early reaction of the kids we know, the people at KidStar are doing an outstanding job of providing radio programming that is for, and much of the time by, kids.

The Children's Corner

KSER 90.7 FM
742-4541
Sunday mornings, 7-9 am

KSER Radio (90.7 FM), a listener supported radio station, presents The Children's Corner, a program of stories, plays, games and songs for young children each Sunday morning from 7-9 am. Programs aired during this time slot include We Like Kids, Pickleberry Pie and KSER's own Enchanted Forest, featuring stories and music by Holly Cummings.

See also: Potluck Musical Variety Show.

Variety Shows

Pied Piper Productions

Mt. Baker Community Club, 2811 Mt. Rainier Dr S, Seattle
722-7209
Season runs fall, winter & spring
Ticket prices: donation of $1.50 per person suggested

After being completely destroyed by fire in 1992, the Mt. Baker Community Center, which hosts Pied Piper Productions, is back in business, offering low-cost, high-quality performing arts for young children and families. This non-profit organization is devoted to presenting quality entertainment for children ages two to seven years and their families. Programs are held on selected Saturday mornings during the fall, winter and spring months and include popular local puppet shows, storytellers, music, dance and sing-alongs. Recent performers include Puppets Please, Allan Hirsch's Alley Oop Show, Carter Family Marionettes, Animal Crackers and Adefua.

Pomegranate at the Village

Village Theatre, 120 Front St N, Issaquah
392-2202
Season runs October-March
Ticket prices: $10-$12

Developed to bring the Eastside community together through performing arts and music, the Pomegranate at the Village entertainment series offers a variety of quality family concerts at the Village Theatre in Issaquah. Recent performers include Eric Tingstad & Nancy Rumbel, the Del McCoury Band and A Fine & Curious Company. Tickets may be purchased as a series or for individual shows.

Potluck Musical Variety Show

Museum of History and Industry, just south of Husky Stadium
543-2710
Saturday mornings, October-May, 11 am
Ticket prices: $5/adults; $3/children 6-12; under 5 are free

Listener-supported KUOW 94.9 FM broadcasts Sandy Bradley's musical variety show live from the Museum of History and Industry each Saturday morning at 11 am. Adults and children of all ages are invited to be part of the broadcast audience and to watch how this lively talk and music show is produced. Arrive by 10:15 or 10:30 am for the warm-up; show starts promptly at 11 am. If you can't make it to the show, tune in to 94.9 FM.

Redmond Children's Playhouse

Redmond Parks & Recreation and Redmond Arts Commission
556-2300
Season runs September- December
Ticket price: $6.50

Every year, September through December, Redmond Parks & Recreation joins the Redmond Arts Commission to present the Redmond Children's Playhouse, a special performing arts series for the entire family. Productions include everything from stage plays to musical performances by popular local talents. Recent performers include Tickle Tune Typhoon, Tim Noah, Missoula Children's Theatre and Seattle Mime Theatre. Tickets may be purchased as a series or for individual shows.

Whoopteedoo!

Bellevue Parks & Recreation, Special Events Office
451-4106
Season runs January-March
Ticket prices: $3.50-$4.50

Bellevue Parks & Recreation

presents a series of performances each winter entitled Whoopteedoo! which are designed especially for children and families. These one- to two-hour shows feature musicians, puppeteers, theatre groups and storytellers, including popular local entertainers such as Tim Noah, Jim Valley and the Rainbow Planet Revue, Tia's Quacker Tunes and the Carter Family Marionettes. Concerts are held at community centers in Bellevue; tickets are available for purchase as a series or individually.

Music

Concerts in the Park

City of Auburn, 931-3043
Bellevue Parks & Recreation, 451-4106
Downtown Seattle Association, 623-0340
Edmonds Parks & Recreation, 771-0228
Everett Parks & Recreation, 259-0300
Federal Way Arts Commission, 661-4050
Kent Parks & Recreation and Arts Commission, 859-3991
Kirkland Parks & Recreation, 828-1217
Lynnwood Arts Commission and Parks & Recreation, 771-4030
Mercer Island Arts Council, 236-3547
Redmond Arts Commission and Parks & Recreation, 556-2300
Seattle Center Mural Concert Series, 684-7200
Woodland Park Zoo's Summer Concert Series, 684-4800

Outdoor concerts are what easy summer living is all about: slowing down the pace and letting the hours drift. The price is right (free), the sound is first-rate and the atmosphere is perfect for kids—they can shake, wiggle and roll all they want. These regularly scheduled events feature a wide variety of music from folk to (soft) rock, and all are family affairs. Some concerts are held at noon on weekdays, but most are on weekend evenings or Sunday afternoons. Go early, bring a blanket and a picnic, then kick back and let the strains of music surround you.

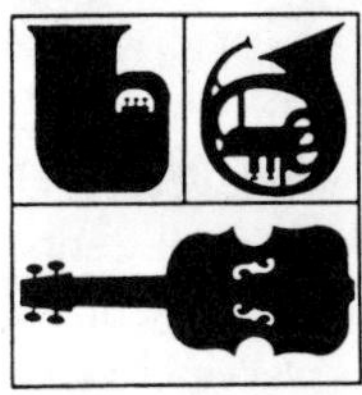

Bellevue Philharmonic Orchestra

455-4171
Season runs October-June
Ticket prices: $11-$14

Founding Conductor/General Manager R. Joseph Scott has done an impressive job developing the Bellevue Philharmonic over the last 25 years. The six pairs of concerts performed each year consistently receive high accolades from audiences and critics alike. Scott demonstrates a strong interest in making orchestral music accessible and appealing to young people—free concert tickets are given away to local schools, and future plans include the organization of a youth orchestra. Concerts are performed at the Westminster Chapel and at several outreach locations in the community.

Chamber Music Play-In
Music Center of the Northwest
783-2798
Throughout the year
Free

Music Center of the Northwest seeks to provide enjoyable musical activities for all ages at little or no cost. Two or three times per year, in the fall, winter and summer months, the center hosts an evening of informal chamber music performances by ensembles of all abilities and ages. The public is invited to drop in to listen or participate—wind, vocal and youth ensembles are especially encouraged to perform. The summer play-in often takes place outdoors in a park with an informal potluck. The Music Center also offers music lessons for children and adults at reasonable cost.

☆ ***Tips***

All seats for Discover Music! are general admission, but purchase tickets early because some shows sell out. Dress is comfortable—despite the Opera House setting. A public parking garage is located across the street, accessible by a covered walkway over Mercer Street.

Discover Music!
Seattle Symphony
443-4747
Season runs October-March
Ticket prices: $5-$7

Each year, the Seattle Symphony Orchestra presents a very popular series of concerts designed to introduce children, ages six to 10 years, to the world of classical music. The one-hour concerts are held Saturday mornings at the Seattle Center's Opera House. Performers are expert at captivating the young audience with entertainment that is cleverly laced with lessons in music basics. Tickets may be purchased as a series or for individual shows.

Musical Experiences
367-6106
Ticket prices: donation of $10/adults, $6/children suggested

Musical Experiences was formed in January 1991 to "further the appreciation and knowledge of music to a broad audience." By presenting a series of short recitals, along with talks about the music being performed, the organization hopes to educate and entertain Seattle audiences in an intimate setting that encourages discussion between the musicians and the audience. The program is directed to adults but might be enjoyed by an older child with some chamber music background.

Once a year, in the late spring, Musical Experiences presents the Young Artists Chamber Music Concert, followed by an entertaining talk about the evening's musical selections. This event provides an excellent opportunity for young children to hear their peers perform.

Northwest Chamber Orchestra
Performances in Kane Hall and Meany Theatre on UW campus, and at Seattle Art Museum
343-0445
Season runs September-May
Ticket prices: $12-$19; children under 17 are admitted free when accompanied by a paying adult

The Northwest Chamber Orchestra has been on the brink of extinction numerous times over its 20-year life, but lucky for us, its music continues to flourish under the baton of conductor Sydney Harth. Each season, the orchestra gives several performances and presents a chamber music series at the SAM auditorium. In contrast to many arts organizations in town, NWCO does more than just talk about getting children culturally involved: it offers free admission to anyone under 17 attending its performances with an adult. The orchestra also performs at elementary schools during the school year and presents a free children's concert every spring.

> ☆ ***Tips***
> *Even though children ages five and up are allowed to sit in the barn at the Olympic Music Festival, most families with young children prefer to bring blankets and relax on the grass outside the barn. Everyone can still enjoy the music, and the kids are free to frolic and pet the animals. Bring your own picnic; pop, espresso, wine and cookies are sold in the milking shed.*

Philadelphia String Quartet
Olympic Music Festival
527-8839
Season runs late June-early September
Ticket prices: $8-$16

The Olympic Music Festival in the Barn series is held on Saturday and Sunday afternoons beginning the last weekend in June through the first weekend in September. Concerts take place on a picturesque 40-acre farm on the Olympic Peninsula. Concert-goers can opt to either sit in the turn-of-the-century barn ($16/adults; $14 children ages 5 and older; ages 5 and under not permitted) or outside on the lawn ($8/person all ages). Each concert starts at 2 pm; gates open at 11 am.

The farm is located 11 miles west of the Hood Canal Bridge, 1/2 mile south of Hwy 104, on Center Rd.

Seattle Chamber Music Festival
Music Under the Stars
328-5606
Season runs late June to late July, every Mon, Wed and Fri, 8 pm
Lakeside School
Ticket prices: $19.50-$21.50 inside St. Nicholas Hall; no charge to sit outside on the grounds

☆ ***Tips***

The Seattle Chamber Music Festival is an extraordinary opportunity to hear fine music for free. The concerts start at 8 pm, but to get settled in a comfortable place, get there between 5 pm and 6 pm. Ticket holders have the option of purchasing catered dinners in advance. Desserts can be purchased, and complimentary coffee and lemonade are available.

Children under six are not allowed in the concert hall, but they are probably better off outside anyway. Concerts last about two hours so be sure to bring plenty of blankets and sweaters if you are sitting outside.

This popular month-long series, started by UW cello professor Toby Saks, is well known for its top-notch performances by local and international talent and for its charming ambiance on the Lakeside School grounds. Now music-loving families can enjoy the concert without paying to sit inside St. Nicholas Hall, thanks to a new system designed to pipe the music out of the hall onto the pastoral campus grounds. Weather permitting, anyone can bring a blanket and picnic and enjoy the music for free, while their children play and dance "under the stars."

Seattle Opera

Seattle Center Opera House
389-7600
Season runs July-May
Ticket prices: $15-$95

A full-length opera is too long for a young child to sit through, but most children are mesmerized by the pageantry and drama of these performances if given in smaller doses. Seattle Opera presents five dazzling operas a year—most playing to sell-out audiences. The best way for your child to access this rich artistic experience is through the Opera Education Department, which offers school programs and opportunities for children to attend dress rehearsals.

Seattle Youth Symphony Orchestra

11065 5th Ave NE, Suite E, Seattle
362-2300
Season runs November-May
Ticket prices: $2-$25

The Seattle Youth Symphony Orchestra's organization comprises over 300 young musicians from the ages of eight to 21, forming three orchestras: the Seattle Debut Symphony (musicians ages eight to 14), the Seattle Junior Symphony (ages 12-16) and the Seattle Youth Symphony (ages 15-21). Each orchestra performs three weekend concerts a year. Under the 20 years of leadership by conductor Vilem Sikol, the Youth Symphony became one of the finest youth orchestras in the country. Since 1988, Sikol's successor, Ruben Guverich, has further raised the performance level. The young

Photo credit: Robert Cole

Young musicians will be inspired by the many music programs and events around the Sound.

performers invariably give first-rate concerts and provide fine role models to inspire the young musician in your family.

University of Washington School of Music
Musicfest
543-4880
Season runs October-June
Ticket prices vary; some concerts are free

The University of Washington School of Music presents a complete season of musical entertainment performed by students, faculty and guest artists. Concerts are held at Meany Theatre and other sites on campus. The series includes voice, instrumental, group and solo performances, including pieces by contemporary artists as well as the masters. Many of the concerts are free of charge, and all are open to the public.

Vocals

Columbia Choirs
Boys Choir, Girls Choir & Youth Choir of East King County
486-1987

Young people ages eight and up who demonstrate the ability to carry a tune and an interest in pursuing music are invited to audition for participation in the Columbia Choirs. Auditions are held in September and January, and

Photo credit: © 1985, Steve Meltzer

The Northwest Girlchoir recently traveled to Austria and Switzerland where they received awards for outstanding achievement.

occasionally in March or April. Children selected receive group voice lessons, learn to read music and perform in concerts and costumed musical productions. All rehearsals are held in the Bellevue and Kirkland area.

The Boys Choir is composed of children ages eight years to "voice change," usually around 14 years; the Girls Choir includes children eight years old through seniors in high school; and the Youth Choir is a co-ed group comprising young people from ninth grade to their freshmen year in college. Members of the choirs perform at a variety of public venues, including senior centers, conventions, weddings and organized park events. Annual public concerts include several holiday concerts in December, as well as winter and spring concerts.

Northwest Choirs

Northwest Boychoir & Northwest Youthchoir

444 NE Ravenna Blvd, Suite 409, Seattle

524-3234

The Northwest Boychoir, Seattle's classic children's choir, is a 50-member all-male group of young people ages eight years to "voice change." The Youthchoir is a co-ed choir open to young people ages 14-17 years. No experience is required to participate in the choirs, just musical aptitude. Auditions for the Boychoir are held in the fall and winter; auditions for the Youthchoir are scheduled throughout the year by appointment only. Annual public performances include "A Festival of Lessons and Carols," held each December, featuring classic Christmas carols and stories of the nativity, as well as audience sing-alongs. This and other concerts are offered to the public free of charge, though freewill offerings are appreciated. The Northwest Choirs also perform sporadic public concerts throughout the year at community events and with other groups such as the Seattle Symphony.

Northwest Girlchoir
728 21st E, Seattle
329-6225

The 270-member Northwest Girlchoir has been performing for Seattle family audiences for nearly 20 years. Annual public performances include three holiday concerts in December and two spring concerts in April. In addition to public concerts and community performances, the Northwest Girlchoir also tours throughout the United States and abroad, recently visiting Austria and Switzerland where they received awards for outstanding achievement. Young people, ages eight to 18, who exhibit a desire to learn and a love of singing are eligible to audition; no experience is necessary. Auditions are held in June and September each year for positions within the five choir levels, ranging from preparatory to advanced.

Seattle Girls' Choir
144 NE 54th St, Seattle
526-1900

The internationally renowned Seattle Girls' Choir and its affiliate choirs, the Everett-Edmonds Girls' Choir, the Kent Valley Girls' Choir, and the Tahoma Girls' Choir, have a total membership of almost 200 young people, ages six to 18 years. The Choir comprises four levels: preparatory, training, intermediate and advanced. The Seattle Girls' Advanced Choir is regarded as one of the top in the world. Auditions are held each year in September, January and May, and are open to anyone between the ages of six and 16. No experience is required. Annual public performances include holiday concerts in December, a winter concert in February or March and a spring concert in May (some of these feature sing-alongs).

Seattle Peace Theatre
4554 12th Ave NE, Seattle
632-5759

Established in 1987, the Seattle Peace Theatre is an organization for young people, ages nine to 19, from throughout the Seattle area, devoted to promoting understanding and cooperation between cultures and countries around the world. The program includes musical theatre classes, an acting company and international exchanges, as well as special choral productions presented each year for the general public. A fall/holiday concert is scheduled each autumn, usually before Thanksgiving; and a spring concert is presented around Mother's Day each year. During the summer months, the Seattle Peace Theatre is busy with international exchanges—one year hosting an international group and the following year visiting a foreign country. Summer productions rotate accordingly.

Storytelling

Stories—whether taken from our cultural traditions, our personal life experiences, or out of favorite books—tell us who we are. They connect us with the past and with each other, which may be why, in the fast-paced '90s, the art form of storytelling is in the midst of an extraordinary revival.

The Seattle Storytellers Guild is one of the strongest of its kind in the United States. Frequent workshops, held throughout the year, provide aspiring storytellers with inspiration and encouragement, and the newsletter is a valuable resource for the flourishing storyteller community. The Guild also presents many opportunities for those who prefer to listen to, rather then tell, a good yarn. Call 621-8646 for information about local storytelling events.

There are many other places in town to take your child to hear a good story. Almost any bookstore that has a strong children's book section offers frequent storytelling sessions. Check out bookstores in the Shopping List to find a store near you.

The King County and Seattle libraries also offer storytelling sessions on a regular basis. Check your local branch for details. (See Essentials.)

Cathy Spagnoli shares a story at Stevens Elementary School, Seattle.

Photo credit: Russell Johnson

Theatre

Bainbridge Performing Arts

Cultural Arts Center,
200 Madison Ave, Bainbridge Island
842-8569
Ticket prices vary

For 35 years, Bainbridge Performing Arts has been an integral part of the Bainbridge Island community, presenting a wide variety of theatre productions, including dramas, musicals and children's favorites. In its new home at the Cultural Arts Center (a short walk from the Winslow ferry), BPA will host such events as theatrical productions, concerts, year-round youth programs for children and teens, as well as performances by the Bainbridge Orchestra.

Bathhouse Theatre

7312 W Green Lake Dr N, Seattle
524-9108
Season runs February-November
Ticket prices: $10-$18

Productions by the Bathhouse Theatre appeal to a broad range of audiences, young and old, with special emphasis on the classics. Two productions each year feature outreach programs for middle and high school students, including special student matinees, workshops and classes, and special curriculum materials for teachers to enhance the theatre experience. The productions are most suitable for older children; the theatre asks that people do not bring infants or young kids who might be disruptive.

Photo credit: Fred Andrews

Ladd Martin (left) and Allen Galli in the Bathhouse Theatre's 1992 production of A Legend of St. Nicholas.

Bellevue School District Youth Theatre

Bellevue School District
455-6019
One production per year
Ticket prices: $6-$10

The Bellevue School District Youth Theatre program offers young people in grades kindergarten through 12, from both public and private schools, an opportunity to experience the creation of a professional production. The students audition in the spring by performing a prepared monologue, song or dance, and those chosen rehearse throughout the summer for performances in the fall. Parents are recruited as well, to handle ticket sales, set construction, chaperone duties, publicity, intermission food sales and other tasks. The costumes are professionally designed but are created by the parents of cast members. Make-up is also handled by a professional, though older cast members and parents are trained to assist. Productions are performed free of charge for students in the Bellevue Public Schools, and reserved-seating public performances are held as well. Bellevue School District Youth Theatre is a non-profit theatre arts program administered by the Bellevue School District.

Civic Light Opera

Jane Addams Theatre
11051 34th Ave NE, Seattle
363-2809
Season runs October-May
Ticket prices: $12-$16

Civic Light Opera celebrated its 15th season of musical theatre in 1992-93, with productions of "The All Night Strut," "Peter Pan," Sweet Charity" and "Carousel." The season runs October through May and includes three to four popular musical productions. Season subscriptions are available, including special Family/Sunday-Only packages. Performances Thursday, Friday, Saturday evenings; Sunday matinees.

Cornish College of the Arts

710 E Roy, Seattle
323-1400
Ticket prices vary

The Cornish Junior Dance Company performs a spring concert for the public during May. The dancers, ages four to 13 years, who have participated in a variety of classes throughout the school year—modern, jazz, ballet and point—combine their accrued skills and talent to perform in this production. In addition, older Cornish students (junior high school age and up) produce music and dance recitals through the year, many of which are held during daytime hours and offered to the general public. Cornish students also perform an outdoor afternoon theatre production at Volunteer Park each year during the spring, which families may enjoy.

Enter Action Theatre

12912 432nd Ave SE, North Bend
888-3287
Ticket prices: $6/adults; $5/children

Enter Action presents three productions a year. One production, especially for kids, is presented annually in early August by young people ages 10 to 20 who have participated in the Kid Action Theatre summer program.

The Generations Theatre

10201 E Riverside Dr, Bothell
487-2441
Season runs November-May
Ticket prices: $4/person in advance; $5/person at the door

Established to bring seniors together with kids, The Generations Theatre in Bothell presents musical stage plays for the entire family. Senior citizens are involved in the set design, ticket sales, make-up, costuming and other backstage positions, as well as acting. The productions, specially designed for children ages three through eight, feature actors young and young-at-heart, performing favorite children's stories, inviting lots of audience participation. School field trips and other groups are welcome; reservations are required. Performances weekdays only.

Intiman Theatre

Intiman Playhouse, Seattle Center
626-0782
Season runs May-October; special holiday production
Ticket prices: $12-$34

After much success with its holiday production in 1992, the Intiman Theatre will make "Peter Pan" an annual event for the entire family. Designed for children ages six and older and their families, this production received rave reviews during its inaugural run. The Intiman's five-show regular season features productions with more mature subject matter designed for adults and teens. Ticket prices range from $12-$24 for the regular season and $14-$34 for the special holiday presentation of "Peter Pan." Special half-price day-of-show tickets for students and seniors are available, as are family subscription packages and group discounts.

Jewish Community Center's Youth Theatre

3801 E Mercer Way, Mercer Island
232-7115
Six or seven productions per year
Ticket prices vary

The Jewish Community Center's Youth Theatre, comprising children in grades three to 12, performs six or seven theatre productions each year for family audiences. These excellent productions are performed by children enrolled in theatre classes at the Community Center and those chosen by audition. The center offers a wide variety of after-school classes in theatre training, including audition technique, ballet, drama, improvisation and street dancing. During the summer months, the Summer Youth Theatre features more intensive workshops in theatre training for children in grades one to nine. Both members and non-members are invited to participate in the classes and productions.

Madrona Youth Theatre
Langston Hughes Cultural Arts Center
104 17th Ave S, Seattle
684-4757
Ticket prices vary

As part of the Langston Hughes Cultural Arts Center, the Madrona Youth Theatre offers a full season of theatrical performances and classes for young people of all ages. The Youth Theatre, comprising young people ages 15 to 25 years, presents several productions during the year for school groups and the general public.

Missoula Children's Theatre
221 E Front, Missoula, Montana 59802
406-728-1911
Tuition and ticket prices vary

Missoula Children's Theatre is a non-profit organization devoted to bringing performing arts to young people throughout the United States and Canada. This unique traveling theatre group is as amazing as it is entertaining. Usually coordinated by local parks departments, arts councils and civic groups, MCT hosts auditions on a given Monday, casting up to 50 local young people, ages kindergarten through grade 12 and older, for parts in one of 10 original musicals in their touring repertoire. No experience or preparation is necessary!

The children begin rehearsals Tuesday and perform Friday, Saturday and, sometimes, Sunday of the same week for the general public. The result is remarkable. In that short period of time, the kids not only learn their lines, but show tremendous poise and professionalism. Recent stops in the Puget Sound area during 1992 included the Redmond, Kent and Bellevue parks departments. MCT is also available for schools or any groups wishing to bring children's theatre to their area. Watch for them in your neighborhood.

Northwest Puppet Center
9123 15th Ave NE, Seattle
523-2579
Season runs October-April
Ticket prices: $4.50/children; $6.50/adults

Northwest Puppet Center, Seattle's only permanent puppet theatre, offers several productions for the entire family each year. Puppet companies from around the world are featured, as are performances by the award-winning

Photo credit: Nothwest Puppet Center

A scene from "The Yellow Dwarf," the Carter Family Marionettes 1993 season opener at the Northwest Puppet Center.

resident company, Carter Family Marionettes. Productions by Northwest Puppet Center are designed with all ages in mind, in a child-friendly environment.

Renton Civic Theatre
507 S 3rd St, Renton
226-5529
Season runs September-August
Ticket prices: $12-$14; $4 discount for children & seniors

Renton Civic Theatre, a professional theatre located in downtown Renton, offers a full season of productions, many of which are suitable for the entire family. RCT includes two or three musicals in its schedule each year, as well as dramas and comedies. Recent productions have included "Peter Pan," "Music Man," and "The Sound of Music." During the summer months, a special kids program for ages six and up is presented, which includes classes and instruction in theatrical arts, culminating in a production performed for the public. The theatre is large and is completely handicapped accessible. A special discount of $4 is offered to seniors and children under 18 for all performances. The productions are most suitable for older children; the theatre asks that people do not bring infants or young kids who might be disruptive.

Seattle Central's Theatre for Children
Performances at The Little Theatre Off-Broadway
1524 Harvard Ave, Seattle
587-5400
Season runs January-April
Ticket prices: $3-$5

Seattle Central Community College's Theatre for Children presents one original production each year, specifically designed for children of all ages. Productions, which have included music, dance, song and mime, always encourage audience participation and are followed by Creative Dramatics Workshops for children. Performances are held on weekday mornings, January through April; reservations are required. School groups are welcome; one adult is admitted free for every ten children.

Seattle Children's Theatre

Charlotte Martin Theatre, Seattle Center
443-0807; ticket office, 441-3322
Season runs October-May
Ticket prices: $8.50/children; $14.50/adults

Rated one of the top children's theatre companies in the United States, Seattle Children's Theatre offers some of the very best in family entertainment. The new Charlotte Martin Theatre at the Seattle Center—Seattle Children's Theatre's new home beginning in September 1993—will offer much of the same intimate ambiance as was present at the Poncho Theatre, SCT's home for the last several years, but with greater seating capacity and increased artistic options. Performances usually run one to two hours in length, including an informative question-and-answer period, during which the audience has a chance to ask questions of the actors themselves—a feature that is a big hit with the younger set.

In addition to its season of theatre productions, the Education Department of Seattle Children's Theatre offers a full array of year-round performing arts classes and workshops for children, teens and adults, as well as teacher programs, school residency programs, and the

Photo credit: © 1993 Chris Bennion

A scene from "Ramona Quimby," one of several highly successful productions that were presented during the '92-93 season at Seattle Children's Theatre.

Young Actors Institute. These outstanding programs are designed to teach and encourage participation in all aspects of the performing arts. Outreach programs, designed for children ages four to 19 years, include a vast array of programs taught by Seattle artists at 34 sites throughout the Puget Sound area. (See In & Around Downtown/ Seattle Center for more information about what the Center has to offer children.)

Seattle Mime Theatre
915 East Pine, Seattle
324-8788

Primarily a touring company, the internationally acclaimed Seattle Mime Theatre travels throughout the Puget Sound region and beyond, bringing its creative productions to schools and private groups. Once or twice a year, the group presents a special performance for the general public at its theatre on Capitol Hill, which is usually suitable for family audiences.

Seattle Puppetory Theatre
13002 10th NW, Seattle
365-0100
Ticket prices vary

Seattle Puppetory Theatre is a touring company of well known puppeteers, who offer performances for children as well as adults. Although its primary focus is on performing for schools, libraries and other private groups, the theatre has also been involved in bringing Japanese puppet companies to Seattle and hopes to bring a company here from Spain in the near future. In addition, Seattle Puppetory Theatre hosts occasional workshops and performances for the general public.

Snoqualmie Falls Forest Theatre & Family Park
36800 SE David Powell Rd, Fall City
624-5225
Season runs June-September
Ticket prices: $11/adults; $10/students & seniors; $4/children 12 & under
Optional salmon or steak dinner, $9 additional

Located just east of Issaquah in Fall City, the Snoqualmie Falls Forest Theatre is committed to presenting family entertainment. Visitors to this outdoor theatre, set within 100 acres of natural forest, will also enjoy a view of Snoqualmie Falls. Two or three productions are presented each summer; future plans include a Saturday afternoon children's production, featuring a box lunch, theatre production and nature walk.

The Mainstage productions are presented at 8 pm on Friday and Saturday evenings, 3 pm on Sunday afternoons. Optional steak or salmon barbecue dinners are served prior to the Friday and Saturday performances and after the Sunday matinee. Reservations are required for dinner and are recommended for all performances. The theatre is a five-minute walk from the free parking area and is accessible for the handicapped.

Village Theatre/Kidstage

120 Front St N, Issaquah
392-2202
Season runs September-June
Ticket prices: $12-$18

Village Theatre presents a season of quality family theatre from September through June, as well as two Kidstage productions that are produced, directed, designed and performed by young people each July and August. The season features musical theatre, drama, comedy and holiday productions. Kidstage, the theatre program for children, offers after-school classes throughout the year for children ages five and up, designed to introduce and encourage participation in the performing arts.

Youth Theatre Northwest

88th Ave SE & SE 40th, Mercer Island
232-2202
Season runs October-May
Ticket price: $6.50

Youth Theatre Northwest on Mercer Island presents a full season of productions designed especially for children ages four years and up and their families. The productions include old favorites as well as original works, dramas and musicals. Young people are involved in all aspects of the productions, including the design and creation of the sets, acting, and directing. Following each performance, the young actors return to the stage for a question-and-answer period with the audience. Youth Theatre also offers a full array of theatre arts classes throughout the year for children, preschool age and older.

CHAPTER 8

Exploring Downtown

Familiarity with a city as an adult and as a parent are two entirely different things. Sometimes it is difficult to pull back and see a neighborhood in terms of what might appeal to children—the sights, shops and snack spots that hold a certain charm for them.

This section is meant to help you discover some of Seattle's most interesting areas *with* your child. You'll discover why visiting an Asian grocery store can be so exciting for a kid. You'll know how to explore the waterfront without wearing out little legs and where to sit down and have a juice box in Pioneer Square. In short, you'll see Seattle in a new light, and realize that though your old haunts are not necessarily ideal for kids, this city has plenty of good alternatives to offer.

Pike Place Public Market

The Pike Place Public Market, located at Pike St and 1st Ave in downtown Seattle, doesn't attract over nine million shoppers a year for its farm fresh goods alone—though these are certainly a main attraction. What does draw people—both residents and tourists—is its very atmosphere. Smack in the midst of downtown, it is one of the least commercial, most diverse areas of Seattle—a place where even the most tight-collared urbanite rubs shoulders with the greenest of earth mothers, without any friction.

Officially opened in 1907, the Market has grown to encompass a wide variety of merchants and wares, plus over a dozen ethnic groceries and bakeries, several restaurants and novelty shops. Though its existence has been threatened twice, once by developers in the early 1970s, and again in the 1980s by hungry investors who wanted to make it more commercial, it has survived and been labeled a Historic District, character intact.

☆ ***Tips***

•Trying to negotiate a stroller through the Market is virtually impossible, because it gets so crowded. Use a front or back pack instead—the kids will be able to see the action more clearly, and you'll be able to move swiftly when the "I want, I want" chants begin.

•The Market hosts the Pike Place Market Festival each year in May, featuring a full weekend of entertainment, special events and hands-on activities for kids (see Season by Season).

•Most Market locations offer the Pike Place Market News, *a complimentary newspaper that contains a good, though slightly outdated map of the Market area.*

•The Market Information Booth, located on 1st Ave and Pike St, offers shopping and restaurant brochures, maps, tour information and discount theatre tickets. It is open daily from 10 am-6 pm.

The Pike Place Market is open daily year-round, Monday-Saturday, 9 am-6 pm; Sunday, 11 am-5 pm (individual merchants may hold slightly different hours; Sunday is a voluntary working day).

The following highlights of the Market are meant to be happened upon rather than sought out—only by strolling the Market and exploring its many nooks and crannies, will your family gain a sense of its offerings and significance to the community.

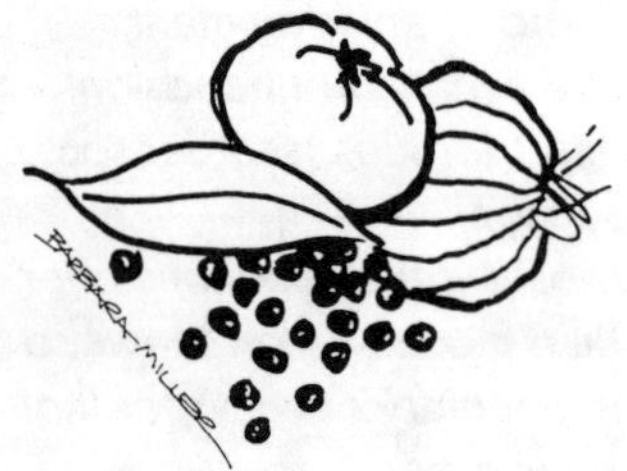

☆ *Essentials*

•Parking can be frustrating in the Market area, especially on sunny summer days. Whatever you do, don't get stuck driving on Pike Place (the road that goes through the Market): Though you might find a parking space, you will surely lose your sanity. Opt for parking in one of the many garages or lots located along Western Ave (the Public Market Parking Garage, just south of Virginia St, has a Skybridge Elevator that provides direct access to the North Arcade).

•Restrooms in the Market are located at the southern and northern points of the Main Arcade, on the First Floor Down Under.

•If you need to get down to the waterfront from the Market, you can take the elevator from the parking garage mentioned above, or take the elevator or stairs located at the southern end of the Market, to Western Ave. Cross the street and follow the stairs down to the waterfront. (See the Pike Place Hillclimb). The stairs do pose a problem for wheelchairs, strollers and cranky kids, so if you just need to get to the waterfront, opt for taking the elevator in the Pike Place Market garage, just north on Western.

Nearby Attractions: Seattle Art Museum, the downtown shopping area, the waterfront.

Highlights

The Pike Place Market is a spectacle in and of itself, but it does have two distinguishing characteristics: a big, red neon clock and *Rachel*—the fat bronze piggy bank that kids love to sit on, pet and stuff with spare change (money collected goes to programs at the Market). The clock and the pig are located where Pike St meets Pike Place.

Pike Place Market Preservation & Development Authority

682-7354

Hours: Monday-Friday, 8:30 am-5:30 pm; Saturday, 8:30 am-3 pm

The Preservation and Development Authority offers tours to school-age children that include the rich history and lore of the Market as well as interesting behind-the-scenes facts and figures.

Shops

Main and North Arcades

The west side of the market, on Pike Place between Pike St and Virginia St

The Main Arcade is easy to find: just listen for the hollering fish mongers and the wet slap of fish being tossed among them. It's an amusing spectacle that was captured on a recent Levis commercial, and one that always attracts a crowd.

There's much more to be seen, however, including colorful rows of fruits and veggies, handmade children's clothing and toys, homemade jams and honeys, seasonal fresh-cut flowers, dried flower arrangements, hand-crafted silver jewelry, pottery, photographs and pictures, unidentifiable junk and lots of action. Many farmers offer samples of their latest products and produce, as well as recipes and information about the locations of their u-pick farms.

This bustling scene, including a variety of musicians, balloon sculptors and other entertainers, is exciting for kids. The man who plays the spoons (forks, spatulas, you name it) is a favorite around the Market.

If you can find enough space to stand still and look down at the floor, you will see the names of the various patrons that gave donations to help replace the Market's old wooden floor in the mid-1980s. There are 46,500 tiles in all—if the kids get bored, have them seek out the one that bears the names of Ron and Nancy Reagan.

First Floor Down Under (the Main Arcade)

Craft Emporium

622-2219

Hours: Mon-Fri, 10 am-5:30 pm; Sat, 10 am-6 pm; Sun, 11 am-5:30 pm

You'll know this shop by the sign outside that reads "Beads Not Bread!" Inside your kids will find trays and trays of beads—metal, glass, porcelain, clay—of all shapes and sizes. Craft Emporium also features different craft materials, such as sequins, glitters, feathers, trimmings, as well as glues and wires. For obvious reasons, this is not a good place to take an orally fixated child.

Golden Age Collectables

622-9799

Summer hours: Mon-Thurs, 10 am-6 pm; Sat, 9:30 am-6 pm; Sun, 11 am-5 pm

Regular hours: Mon-Thurs, 10 am-5:30 pm; Fri, 10 am-6 pm; Sat, 9:30 am-6 pm; Sun, 11 am-5 pm

Golden Age Collectables is stuffed full of comic books, modern and old, for children and adults (be forewarned that some of the material is not at all appropriate for kids). Also featured are baseball and other sports cards, signed baseballs, models, books and Star Trek memorabilia.

House of Jade

622-9392

Hours: Mon-Sat, 10 am-5 pm

An ideal store for older children who collect trinkets, figurines, touristy items, and other useless junk.

Market Coins
624-9681
Hours vary

Lots of old baseball cards, stamps and coins for the serious and amateur collectors in the family.

Market Toys and Gifts
624-4356
Hours: Mon-Sat, 11 am-5 pm

The play table and "This is a touch shop" plaque are more than subtle hints that kids are welcome in this shop, which makes up for the fact that the inventory is not all that interesting.

MysterE Books
622-5182
Hours: Mon-Sat, 9:30 am-5:30 pm; Sun 10 am-5 pm

A small but well-stocked bookstore with a good children's book section located at the back on the right.

Pike Place Gifts
223-9430
Hours: daily, 10 am-6 pm

This shop specializes in Seattle t-shirts, baseball caps, mugs and other tourist paraphernalia.

Pike Place Market Magic Shop
MAGIC 71 (624-4271)
Hours: Mon-Sat, 10 am-6 pm

An authentic magic shop that sells a wide variety of supplies for every level of magician. You'll find everything from gags to juggling supplies, rubber chickens to ventriloquist dummies, puzzles to books and videos. Performances by professional musicians, mimes and jugglers are a regular occurrence at this store, and the staff are more than willing to show what's up their own sleeves.

Wisdom Marionettes
527-9124
Hours: daily, 11 am-4 pm

A booth right next to the magic shop, which features handmade marionettes of all kinds, including dinosaurs, eagles, cyclops and martians, as well as finger and rod puppets. Impromptu puppet shows have been known to occur here.

Second Floor Down Under

Grandma's Attic
682-9281
Regular hours: Mon-Fri, 10:30 am-5:30 pm; Sat, 10 am-6 pm; Sun, 10:30 am-5:30 pm

Ideal stop for two purposes: augmenting the "dress-up box" and decorating a doll house. Grandma's Attic sells frocks, ties, wigs, petticoats, shoes and other vintage items for dress-up (or hip high school wardrobes), and a nice selection of reasonably priced miniatures.

Nook & Cranny
622-4709
Hours: Mon, Thurs, Fri, Sat, 10:30 am-4:30 pm

Raggedy Ann and Andy and all their relatives inhabit Nook & Cranny, as do 1960s Barbies and other collectable toys.

If your kids are into scales more than feathers, visit the lower level of the Seattle Market Parrot and Reptile House.

Shakespeare & Co.

624-7151

Hours: daily, 10:30 am-5:30 pm

Far from the left bank of the Seine, this Shakespeare & Co. carries some older, hard-cover children's books for reasonable prices, as well as an eclectic collection of books for the older reader.

Silly Old Bear

623-2325

Hours: Mon-Sat, 10:30 am-5 pm

Aptly named, this charming little store carries all sorts of stuffed bears and bear stuff. Other merchandise includes gnomes, miniatures, little books, tea sets, blocks and stickers.

Mezzanine Level

The Candy Store

625-0420

Hours: daily, 10:30 am-5:30 pm

This place looks more like a junk shop than a candy store. A quick sampling, however, verified that the candy is fresh and sweet as ever. A good place to get cotton candy and gum cigars.

Seattle Market Parrot & Reptile House

1500 Western Ave

467-6133

Hours: Mon-Sat, 10 am-6 pm; Sun, 12-5 pm

This small and crowded co-op at the base of Pike Place Market should not be missed if you are with school-age children, despite the $.50 browsing fee for non-member browsers (money collected supposedly goes to feeding the birds and critters and will be refunded if you make a purchase). Upstairs you will be greeted by the screaming caws and tweety-bird pips of a variety of different birds, including parrots, canaries and finches. Remind your child not to put his fingers anywhere near the cages—some of these birds' beaks look downright menacing.

If your kids are more into scales than feathers, take them downstairs to the reptile room, where they can feast their eyes on such natural marvels as pythons, iguanas and lizards. Point out the fuzzy King Baboon Tarantula (it's bigger than even its name would imply), the

Tomato Toad (guess what color it is) and the price tags—just in case they are getting any ideas about leaving with a cuddly new family pet.

Economy Row

Just south of Main Arcade, running east/west from Pike Place to First Ave

Stamp Happy

682-8575

Hours: daily, 9:30 am-5:30 pm

This tiny stand sells personalized stamps, rubber stamps, etc.

Economy Market Atrium

Just south of Pike St, accessible from 1st Ave or Economy Row

The Great Wind-Up

621-9370

Hours: Mon-Sat, 10 am -5 pm; Sun, 12-4 pm

The employees of The Great Wind-Up do more than ring up the sales—they keep about a dozen toys flipping, barking, walking and hopping. The store claims to have the largest collection of wind-up and animated toys in the Northwest, a number of which can be tested on a counter exclusively for this purpose. The only problem is that the counter is high, even for an adult, so young kids will have to be lifted up to play (a clever ploy to make sure that patrons supervise their kids). The rest of the store has very specific signs posted, stating what kids can and cannot touch. Look for the talking mirrors, the dinosaur slippers and the creeping forearm.

Post Alley Market

Opposite the Main Arcade, across Pike Place, Post Alley starts mid-block and cuts toward Pine St

Emerald Earth Toys

447-9566

Hours: daily, 9 am-6 pm

This small shop boasts a large selection of scientific, educational and culturally diverse toys and games for all ages.

Snacks

Biringer Farm, Bakery and Country Store

Post Alley Market

467-0383

Hours: Mon-Sat, 8 am-6 pm; Sun, 9 am-5 pm

If anyone in the family likes berries, this place has the best berry milkshakes and cobblers around. Biringer Farms also sells bagels, pot pies, muffins, scones, soups and treats, as well as scone mix, teas, sauces and syrups.

Burrito Express

1st Ave, just south of Economy Row

623-3619

Hours: daily, 10 am -5 pm

Always a long line at this take-out lunch spot that makes yummy fresh burritos "from scratch" and without lard.

Chocolate & Ice Cream Delight

Soames-Dunn Building (opposite the North Arcade, midway between Stewart & Virginia streets on Pike Place)
441-8877
Hours: Mon-Sat, 9 am-6:30 pm; Sun, 12-6 pm

An ice cream fountain that offers all the rich traditional treats, as well as delicious frozen yogurt.

The Crumpet Shop

Corner Market Building (northwest corner of 1st Ave and Pike St)
682-1598
Hours: Mon-Fri, 7:30 am-5 pm; Sat, 7:30 am-5:30 pm

Features a selection of teas, crumpets, muffins, preserves and other treats. With over 40 different crumpet toppings from which to choose (from jam to green eggs), everyone in the family should be sated. Some outside seating available (one table and three chairs, to be exact). A crumpet with butter and jam and a cup of tea runs about $1.75.

DeLaurenti's Pizza Window

Economy Row and 1st Ave, across from newsstand
622-0141
Hours: Mon-Sat, 11 am-5 pm

Delicious to-go pizza slices starting at $1.25. Stop by their adjoining store if you need any Italian delicacies, including a wonderful deli counter, replete with fresh Tuscan baguettes, cheeses and meats, a fine selection of olive oils and other specialties.

Popcorner

Post Alley Market
622-4240
Hours: Mon-Sat, 10 am-6 pm; Sun, 12-5 pm

Never mind boring old butter and salt! The Popcorner goes corn-crazy with such flavorings as strawberry, pina colada, chocolate and bubblegum. Sold by the bag or by the tin, prices start at $1.99.

Rasa Malaysia

Sanitary Market (opposite the Main Arcade, north of the Corner Market Building)
624-8388
Hours: Mon-Fri, 11 am-6 pm; weekend hours vary

Rasa Malaysia's take-out counter serves up delicious noodle and vegetable dishes, as well as tasty barbecued pork and chicken. Prices are $3-$4.50 per dish.

Three Girls Bakery

Sanitary Market
622-1045
Hours: Mon-Sat, 7 am-6 pm

Three Girls Bakery bakes their own breads and other goodies and makes some of the best, biggest sandwiches in town. Don't bother trying to get a counter seat with the kids, it is much too popular, especially at lunch time.Soups are also delicious, as is the lemonade.

Pike Place Hillclimb

On the long climb up the stairs connecting the waterfront to the Pike Place Market, there are several interesting places to stop and catch your breath.

City Kites/City Toys

622-5349

Hours: Mon-Fri, 10:30 am-5:30 pm; Sat, 10 am-5:30 pm; Sun, 11 am-5:30 pm

One of the most fun and colorful shops in the area, City Kites/City Toys sells the kinds of things that every child—and most adults—find irresistible: flying objects, bathtub friends, plastic creatures and zany whats-its. The open, uncluttered layout of the store, with its several hands-on play stations, is superb for young visitors, and the staff, who are everywhere, are always helpful and humorous. City Kites/City Toys also has a good selection of activity books, including the very popular Klutz Press series.

El Puerco Lloron

624-0541

Hours: Mon-Thurs, 11:30 am-8 pm; Fri & Sat, 11:30 am-9 pm; Sun, 12-6:30 pm

This little spot serves some of the most authentic, tasty and reasonably priced Mexican food in the city. Finding a place to sit is a trick; send someone ahead to grab a table while you get in the cafeteria line to get the food.

Procopio Gelateria Italian Ice Cream

622-4280

Hours: Mon-Thurs, 9 am-10 pm; Fri & Sat, 9 am-12 am; Sun, 10 am-10 pm

Wake up your taste buds with a dollop of sorbet in vivid fruit flavors.

The Waterfront Streetcar will take you along the waterfront, through Pioneer Square, past the Kingdome and to the edge of the International District.

Photo credit: Paul Dowling

The Waterfront

On the Seattle downtown waterfront you'll find the good, the bad and the ugly. Stand out on Pier 62 facing Elliott Bay and feast your eyes on the sparkling waters and the glorious Olympic Mountains beyond. Remind your kids that over one hundred years ago the Native Americans used this very spot for landing their boats. Notice the bustling sea-going traffic and the picturesque ferries. Now turn around and behold the ugly—the Alaskan Way Viaduct, a dinosaur of a freeway that crudely interrupts downtown's graceful slope to the water and serves as a hideous and noisy testimony to the price of urban non-planning. The bad side of this strip that marries land to sea is the endless assortment of shops filled with mounds of schlock. But don't be discouraged; despite this area's helter-skelter development, or perhaps because of it, there is plenty to see and do here with kids. The Seattle Waterfront is a splendid place to spend an afternoon, and if being close to the water just isn't enough, you can extend your adventure by hopping on one of the ferries or boats taking off from the various piers.

If you think your fellow explorers have the stamina, the best way to see the waterfront is to ride the Waterfront Streetcar (commonly called the trolley) one direction and then stroll back. On your promenade you'll find thought-provoking public art, countless shops, maritime traffic to distract and entertain, and plenty of tasty food and invigorating salt air.

The most interesting segment of the waterfront extends from the south end at Pier 48 (at the base of Washington St) to the north end at Pier 70 (at the base of Broad St). If you have a budding sea captain in the house, it may be worth going a bit further to the more industrial Pier 36, where you'll find a Coast Guard Vessel Traffic Center (286-5640) and Coast Guard Museum (286-9608). Whatever you decide, there are a couple different approaches to exploring this area, depending on how much walking you care to do. One suggestion is to park your wheels near the base of

☆ *Tips*

Watch kids extra carefully when walking the Seattle Waterfront: The guardrails next to the water are not childproof.

You may view the endless tourist shops as pure torment, but many school-age kids are in bliss if they can putter around a store full of cute and useless items. Be sure to clearly spell out the shopping budget before you get inside the first store. (A zero shopping budget is probably the most relaxing for everybody.) If you have a young child who is at that stage where he rejoices in seizing fragile items and flinging them onto the floor, skip the shops and go straight to the carousel (Pier 57), the aquarium or the ferry dock.

The half-mile walk between Pier 48 and Pier 59 covers the most interesting and entertaining segment of this area. If you decide to head further north to Pier 70's shops or Myrtle Edwards Park, either prepare yourself and the kids for a rather boring walk, or jump aboard the trolley.

the Pike Place Hillclimb, across the street from the Seattle Aquarium (Pier 59), and then climb aboard the southbound trolley at the Pike station. Disembark at the Washington St station and cross the road to Pier 48—about a half-mile walk from your car (to visit Pier 36, get off the trolley at Main St). If you would prefer, you can park at the north end at Pier 70, by Myrtle Edwards Park, ride the trolley the length of the waterfront and extend your walk back by another half mile.

Though you're sure to occasionally sink deep into touristville on your waterfront tour, you will just as often be charmed by the beauty and rich history of this area and amazed at its outstanding offerings: a first-rate aquarium, several charming parks and countless stunning vistas.

☆ *Essentials*

Metro's bright green Waterfront Streetcar offers connections between Pier 70 and the International District, with nine stops along the way. You can ride along the waterfront on Alaskan Way to Main St, through Pioneer Square to the edge of the International District at 5th Ave & S Jackson. The kids will love the noise and commotion of the ride. If you plan to get off the streetcar and then on again within an hour, ask the conductor for a transfer, which will allow you to board another streetcar along the way without paying additional fares. The conductors are very helpful with information on what sites are located at each stop and directing you to your destination. The Waterfront Streetcar operates daily year-round every 20-30 minutes; seasonal hours vary. Adult fares are: non-rush hour, $.85; rush-hour, $1.10. Child fare is $.75 at all times.

If fatigue sets in on your outing, you can hitch a ride on Casual Cabs—bicycle cabs that cover the waterfront and Pioneer Square area. Prices run around $1-$2 per kid and $4-$5 for adults, but the drivers are willing (expect) to negotiate the rate.

Parking is available at the meters that run along under the Alaskan Way Viaduct, but have your quarters handy: cost is $1.50 for two hours and meters only take quarters. Thanks to the downtown merchants' protests about recent meter rate increases, there is some reprieve for weekend shoppers: two hours of free meter parking on Saturdays (Sundays are always free). There are also several parking lots on Western Ave, one block off the waterfront, and a parking garage across the street from the Aquarium that is handy if you plan to use the Hillclimb stairs to extend your tour to the Pike Place Market.

Pier 48

At this Washington St Public Boat Landing, take the time to look over the fine totem pole that sits inside the park and to read the historical plaques on the guard railings. Did you know Dr. Alexander De Soto had his Wayside Mission Hospital for the destitute on this site from 1900-1909?

Pier 50-Pier 53

Pier 50 marks the beginning of Colman Dock, the terminal for ferries to Bremerton on the Kitsap Peninsula, Bainbridge Island and (passenger only) Vashon Island.

Just north of the terminal on Pier 53 sits Fire Station #5, home port for two magnificent fireboats, the Alki and the Duwamish. On summer days you might see the fireboats out in the bay spraying their hoses up towards the sky in a majestic waterworks display (the Duwamish pumps 22,000 gallons a minute).

☆ ***Tips***

Parking the car and walking on the Seattle to Bainbridge ferry is a great outing with a kid (and a fine way to show off Seattle to out-of-town visitors). The ride is an easy 30 minutes, and the town of Winslow is a short stroll from the ferry dock. Take a morning ferry and enjoy a scrumptious breakfast at the Streamliner Diner (397 Winslow Way E, 842-8595). There's a Winslow farmers market every Saturday, May-October.

Highlights

Washington State Ferries

464-6400 or (800) 843-3779
Operate year-round
Schedules & rates vary for each route

Operating the largest ferry system in the United States, the Washington State Ferries system connects island and peninsula communities throughout the Puget Sound region. Colman Dock at Pier 52 is home for the Bainbridge, Bremerton and Vashon (passenger-only) routes. Passengers can ride aboard a variety of boats within the fleet, from the smallest passenger-only ferry, which carries 250 people, to the jumbo ferry, which carries 2,000 people and 206 cars! The shortest ride is the Fauntleroy (West Seattle) to Vashon Island run. The longest ride is the Seattle to Bremerton run, which lasts just about one hour.

☆ *Essentials*

Passengers are welcome to bring their own food on board or enjoy something from the cafeteria (the food is quite good and reasonably priced). There is even a children's meal offered, much like the Happy Meal from McDonald's, packaged in a 'ferry box' to take home.

Pier 54-Pier 57

At Pier 54 the tourist shops begin in earnest. If you are determined not to shop, either walk briskly or jump on a tour boat. Otherwise, summon up your patience and take the kids in for some fun browsing.

Highlights

Seattle Harbor Tours

Departs from Piers 55 & 57
Cruise the Locks,623-1445; $9-$19
One-Hour Harbor Tour, 623-1445; $5-$11
Lake Washington Cruise, 623-1445; $5-$14
Children under 5 are free for all tours
Call to confirm seasonal departure times
Group rates available

You don't need out-of-town guests to embark on a boat tour of the city. Kids will delight in going under, rather than over, familiar bridges and picking out landmarks they have grown accustomed to viewing from a different angle. The narratives are lively and informative

Seattle Harbor Tours offer a different view of familiar surroundings.

— even native Seattleites will probably learn something new about their home town.

The two-and-one-half hour Cruise the Locks tour is the most interesting of the three excursions offered by Seattle Harbor Tours, the highlight being a trip through the Hiram M. Chittenden Locks. You'll also cruise through Lake Union, the Fremont cut, Shilshole Bay, around West Point and Elliott Bay to Pier 57 on the Seattle Waterfront, plus take a 15-minute ride aboard a motor coach between Chandler's Cove on Lake Union and Pier 57. Tours depart daily year-round from Pier 57.

The Harbor Tour is a one-hour trip along the Seattle Waterfront through Elliott Bay, including the shipyards and Duwamish Waterway. This route offers a fascinating look at the downtown waterfront—a central part of Seattle's identity that is easily overlooked when traveling by land. Tours depart daily year-round from Pier 55.

For a trip through the serene waters of Lake Washington, take the Lake Washington cruise aboard the Queen's Launch. The one-and-one-half-hour tour provides a look at the affluent residential developments that lie along the east side of the lake as you travel along the Kirkland shoreline, Yarrow Point, Medina and Meydenbauer Bay. A quick crossing to the western shores gives a water view of Husky Stadium at the University of Washington, along with some interesting narrative about the two floating bridges that cross the lake. (There are some lucky commuters who use their private boats to travel to work everyday from the Eastside to the University.) Tours depart from Kirkland's Marina Park, all seasons except winter.

Tillicum Village Tour

Departs from Piers 55 & 56
443-1244
Operates year-round; seasonal departure times vary
Ticket prices: $7.95-$39.95; children 3 & under are free

Just eight miles from Seattle in Puget Sound lies Blake Island, a Washington State Park featuring nearly 500 acres of natural forest and beaches, and Tillicum Village. For over 30 years, tourists and residents alike have visited this little island to experience a Northwest Native tradition. Some adults are put off by the "touristy" style of the tour, but most school-age children consider the trip a fun and memorable treat.

The four-hour Tillicum Village Tour departs from the Seattle Waterfront for an eight-mile trip across Puget Sound on one of the Goodtime boats. Before you speed off to Blake Island, you're treated to a narrated tour of Elliott Bay and the city's busy port facilities.

Once you reach the island, you head for Tillicum Village's huge cedar longhouse, where a complete salmon dinner—baked over an alderwood fire—awaits you. Following dinner, you and your family are treated to a Tillicum Village Native American production, featuring the music, dance and legends of the Northwest Coast Indians.

On select days between May and September, Tillicum Village offers a Hiker Special, featuring an additional two-and-one-half hours of time on the island to explore 16 miles of hiking trails. Wildlife is abundant on Blake Island, with over 50 deer as well as eagles and mink. Additional attractions include a gift shop, five miles of beaches, cultural displays, and arts and crafts. Reservations are recommended.

Ye Olde Curiosity Shop

Pier 54
682-5844
Hours: open daily, 9 am-9 pm in the summer; 9:30 am-6 pm, Oct-Apr

On your waterfront stroll you are

not likely to find crusty old sailors with parrots spinning alluring tales of exotic places. But you can give your child a glimpse of the bizarre and mysterious world that lies out there with a visit to Ye Olde Curiosity Shop on Pier 54. Since 1899, this one-of-a-kind place has fascinated waterfront visitors, and your child will probably be talking about it long after you go home. Don't be put off by all the souvenir stuff—you have to look carefully to spot the weird attractions that make this a place for the curious indeed. If you don't find the fully dressed fleas, two shrunken heads, two (real) mummies and a bean that will hold 10 ivory elephants, you are not looking carefully enough.

Snacks/Restaurants

Ivar's Acres of Clams

Pier 54
624-6852

Enjoy tasty fish and chips and chowder outside under cover (be ready to share with the seagulls) or go inside for a delicious salmon meal (see Basics/Restaurants). The kids will like the sculpture of Ivar and his friends, the seagulls, that sits just outside the take-out fish bar.

Red Robin Express

Pier 55
624-3969

Buy an exceptionally good burger to take outside and enjoy at a table on the pier. If you want a wider selection, dine inside—Red Robin has a very good children's menu.

The Frankfurter

Pier 55
622-1748

The hot dogs and thirst-quenching fresh-squeezed lemonade are the best in the city. Take-out only.

DEE-LICIOUS!

Shops

Waterfront Landmark

Pier 55
622-3939

For just $.50, your kids can take home a scoop of the beautifully colored rocks and tiny shells that can be found in the front of this shop. Delicious fudge is made and sold in the rear of the store, so depending on your parental position on candy, either head for, or steer clear of, this area.

Jonah's Glass Shop

Pier 55
624-2558

Very pretty. Very, very fragile. For under-control kids only.

Pier 57-Pier 59

The Pavilion on Pier 57 is home to several shops, the Seattle Sourdough Baking Company (which sells delicious breads) and to an unsuspecting child's delight, a grand old carousel (if only it could be outside). Merry-go-round rides are $1, and popcorn, cookies and drinks are sold nearby. Booths that brim with goods from all over the world surround the carousel for your consuming pleasure.

Waterfront Park on Pier 59 has ample space to run (no grass) and plenty of places to sit. With an unparalleled view of the water and mountains, it is a fine place to rest and revive before visiting the outstanding Seattle Aquarium, located just to the north. Note the plaque on the railing above the park commemorating the landing of the boat the *Portland* in 1897. It was loaded with about two tons of gold from the Klondike and lit the fuse for the gold rush that was to blast Seattle out of its early economic slump.

Access to the Pike Place Market via the stairs—called the Pike Place Hillclimb—is across the street from the north end of the Aquarium. There's also an elevator in the parking garage near the stairs that will take you to the Market.

Highlights

The Seattle Aquarium

Pier 59
386-4320

See Animals, Animals, Animals for details.

Omnidome Theatre

Pier 59
622-1868

See Seattle Aquarium in Animals, Animals, Animals for details.

Snacks/Restaurants

The Salmon Cooker

Pier 57
622-1748

Located just outside the Pavilion. The alder-smoked fish smells better than it tastes, but the muffins, brownies and cookies sold across the way are delicious.

Pavilion Food Court

Pier 57

If someone in your group hankers for something other than fish, chips, burgers and dogs, check out the take-out restaurants on top of the Pavilion on Pier 57. Choices include Mexican, Chinese and teriyaki.

Steamers
Pier 59
624-0312

A good place to grab fish and chips before you go into the Aquarium or the Omnidome.

Pier 62-Pier 63

In 1989, the Seattle Arts Commission and the Department of Community Development and Parks and Recreation jointly recommended Piers 62 and 63 be designated as one open public space. It has since become the site of the popular "Concerts on the Dock" series held every summer (Carole King, B.B. King, Neville Brothers, etc. Call Ticketmaster, 628-0888, for information).

On a chain link perimeter fence that frames the area, look for a series of questions that are part of the public artwork that was commissioned by the local Arts Commission. Painted in red, directly on the fence, the questions appear and disappear depending on the viewer position and the condition of the light, sky and water. See if you and your kids can find (and answer!) the following: Who salutes longest? Who follows orders? Who laughs last? What remains? What disappears? Who decides? Who does the time? Who speaks?

After that flurry of intellectual stimulation, let the kids run with abandon in the wide-open space, while you soak in the magnificent view.

This is a good place to end your walking tour if your group is running out of steam. Beyond this point there is not much of interest until you get down to Pier 70 (more shops and restaurants) and Myrtle Edwards Park.

Pier 66-Pier 70

At Pier 66 you'll see construction underway. A major new development is in the works, which will include a maritime museum and a conference center.

At Pier 70 the shopping and snacking may be resumed. This lovely old building, which was built in 1910 as a terminal for ocean liners, will not get the attention it deserves if you started out at Pier 48! If you are at all up for it, and the kids aren't too crabby, browse through Pier 1 Imports. Then head over to Myrtle Edwards Park for a refreshing stroll to complete your waterfront tour.

Highlights

Victoria Clipper
Pier 69
448-5000
Fares vary according to the season: round trip adult $74-$85; child fare is half the adult fare. With a 14-day advance purchase, cost for adults is $59-$69. Packages that include hotel are available.

If you decide to take the Clipper

boat to Victoria, B.C., your trip will begin at the new port building on Pier 69. Victoria is a fabulous place to visit with a school-age child, either for a day or overnight. There is plenty to see and do within easy walking distance of the harbor, where the Clipper will arrive. (Watch out for the truly gruesome Chamber of Horrors at the Royal London Wax Museum located near the harbor).

It is worth going to Victoria for a day with your children just to be able to take them to the outstanding Royal British Columbia Museum (604/387-3701) located a half block away from the Clipper terminal. It is one of the finest natural and historical museums you will ever visit. On the second floor you'll walk through spectacular dioramas of the seacoast, a coastal rain forest and the Fraser River delta. Up on the third-floor history section there are full-scale working models of a sawmill, coal mine and gold-sluicing operation, as well as a full-scale Victorian town. The reconstructed hull of Captain George Vancouver's H.M.S. *Discovery* is astonishing in its realism. Also on the third floor, is an outstanding exhibit on native Canadian history and culture, including totem poles and a longhouse. The museum is open daily except Christmas and New Year's Day. Cost is $5 adults; $1 children ages 6-11, under 6 free.

Restaurants

Old Spaghetti Factory
2801 Elliott
441-7724

See Basics/Restaurants.

Photo credit: Paul Dowling

The bronze Cow & Dog sculpture by Brad Rude can be found at the south end of Occidental Mall in Pioneer Square.

Pioneer Square

The history of Pioneer Square is one of the more interesting tales of Seattle, one that will likely prompt even the most distracted youngster to stand still and listen, for at least 30 seconds. From the city's incorporation in 1869 to the late 1880s, it was a thriving business district, where most of Seattle's 40,000 residents lived and worked. But on June 6, 1889, a furniture maker in the area left a pot of glue on a hot stove unattended, resulting in the biggest fire in Seattle's history—one that burned the young city to ashes in mere hours.

The real capper of the story (sure to keep your child's attention for an additional 15 seconds) is that you and your family can still visit the Seattle of the late 1800s—at least what remains of it! Because of the Great Fire, and a poorly planned sewage system, the community decided to rebuild the city atop the old one—in effect, raising street level by one story. The old city is still accessible (by tour) and can be seen through some of the sidewalk grates in the area.

Today, Pioneer Square is one of Seattle's most diverse and architecturally impressive areas—a neighborhood full of landmarks, galleries, funky shops and restaurants. It extends from the Kingdome in the south to Cherry St to the north, and from Alaskan Way east to 2nd Ave, encompassing some of the most exquisite architecture (of stone, brick and other nonflammable materials) in the whole of Seattle. Don't forget to look up when walking around Pioneer Square—the art extends far above eye level.

☆ *Essentials*

There are plenty of parking meters and parking lots, which often fill up if there's an event at the Kingdome. You may want to leave your car along the waterfront; you can catch the Waterfront Streetcar to Pioneer Square's South Main St from as far north as Pier 70.

☆ ***Tips***

•During the summer months, an information booth in Pioneer Square at Occidental S and S Main is open from 10 am-4 pm, Monday through Saturday, offering directions, suggestions and literature about the area.

•Don't be caught off guard by the number of panhandlers in Pioneer Square. Seattle's bicycle police keep an eye out for any trouble—you shouldn't feel intimidated. Local businesses have launched a fairly successful campaign over the past few years, asking the community not to give money to these transients. You'll likely support a bad habit instead of a worthy cause. Give instead to charities or missions that help the homeless.

•If you and the little ones are exploring on foot, note that 1st Ave gets pretty boring south of Occidental, and the scene gets slightly scary between Second Ave and the International District.

Highlights

Kingdome

201 South King St.
296-DOME; ticket office recording, 296-3111

Also known as the King County Domed Stadium, this covered sports arena has become somewhat of a landmark, though some would wonder why: It looks like a gigantic, new-fangled citrus juicer. Moreover, it lacks good acoustics and a convertible top. That about covers its most commonly heard criticisms.

In its favor, the Kingdome has provided a home for the Seattle Mariners and the Seahawks, and a location for several events and festivals year-round.

For the sports fans in your family, the Kingdome offers behind-the-scenes group and private tours of a locker room, the working press box, VIP areas, the field level and the Kingdome Sports Museum. Visitors will learn how playing surfaces are changed for basketball, football and baseball and much more. Drop-in public tours are offered Monday through Saturday at 11 am, 1 pm and 3 pm, mid-April through mid-September. Prices range from $1.25-$3 per person. Call 296-3128 for more information.

Klondike Gold Rush National Historical Park

117 S Main, Seattle
553-7220
Open daily, 9 am-5 pm
Free admission

This little museum, set up by the National Park Service, documents the Gold Rush of the late 1800s through a number of different media. See Kid Culture/Exhibits and Museums.

Occidental Mall

Between S Main and S Jackson on Occidental

This red-bricked pedestrian mall is lined with galleries, offices, restaurants and trees. Kids love to pet the bronze Cow & Dog sculpture near the south end. The information booth mentioned in "Tips" can be found at the north end of the mall.

Occidental Park

Between S Main and S Washington on Occidental

Situated right in the center of this historical district, across from Occidental Mall, this cobblestoned area is the site of summer concerts and the Seattle Fire Festival in June (see Season by Season). Central to its decor are a pergola, several benches and four totem carvings, including *Tsonqua* (a welcoming spirit) and the tall, thick *Sun and Raven* pole. Although the transient population here may be intimidating on some days, it is a safe, populated and open space to sit down and have a rest, while the kids run off extra steam.

Pioneer Place

Corner of Yesler and James streets,

Here's where the word "pioneer" really comes into play. This triangular area, adorned with a 1905 pergola, marks Seattle's first settlement.

Seattle Fire Department Headquarters

Corner of 2nd Ave S and S Main
386-3111

Although it may be tempting to take your future firefighter in to see the shiny red trucks, this station is not set up to handle drop-in guests.

If you happen to be passing by, however, tell your kids to check out the metal one-dimensional sculptures of firefighters that decorate the exterior corners of the building. Group tours of the station can be arranged in advance by calling the above phone number.

Smith Tower

2nd Ave S and Yesler Way
682-9393
Hours: Mon-Fri, 9-11 am, 1:30-4:30 pm, 5:30-10 pm, except during events; Sat-Sun, 9 am-10 pm
Admission: $2/adults; $1/children 12 & under and seniors (65+); children under 6 free.

The 42-story Smith Tower was built between 1911 and 1914, and was, at that time, the tallest building west of the Mississippi. The entire building was constructed with various stones and metals, in a pryophobic attempt to make the building fire resistant.

When you walk into the lobby, direct your child's attention to the ornate Native American busts that line the ceiling. Then buy tickets to the observation deck from the attendant of Elevator No. 8 (the one nearest the building's entrance), and get ready for one of the best elevator rides in Seattle.

The attendant will give you a brief run down of the Smith Tower's history on the way up, but your kids will likely be more captivated by his actions than his words. This is a true, old-fashioned elevator—metal gate and all—run not by pushing buttons, but by maneuvering a brass lever. The shaft and pulley are visible from inside—a thrilling sight for aspiring engineers. When you get out on the 35th floor, look to the right of the elevator, and you will see the Otis elevator motor that just pulled you up—"one of the eight similar machines operating the high-speed passenger elevators in the building."

The Chinese Room is an elegant albeit stark room, with a red carpeted floor and an ornately carved and painted ceiling. A few substantial pieces of sculpted furniture and an exquisite view fill the rest of the room. To access the observation deck, use the sliding glass doors at the north end of the room.

Underground Tour

Begins at Pioneer Place
Ticket prices: $4.75/adults; $3.50/ students & seniors; $2.25/children 6-12; children 5 & under are free
682-4646

This tour takes you beneath Pioneer Square to see what's left of 1889 Seattle. As stated previously, Pioneer Square was literally rebuilt over the old city, after the Great Seattle Fire of 1889. The tours are offered daily, year-round, and include many interesting historical facts (as well as several corny jokes). Reservations are suggested, as tours fill quickly; advance reservations are required for groups. The tour runs about one-and-a-half- hours and is not wheelchair or stroller accessible. Be warned that some kids don't find this tour at all interesting—it requires a penchant for history, a vivid imagination and an appreciation of subterranean scents and scenes.

Waterfall Park

Corner of S Main and 2nd Ave S, across from the Fire Station

The site of the original offices of United Parcel Service, this small fenced park provides a nice, cool setting for a snack. The park's main feature is (yep) a waterfall—use it as a bargaining tool, if you want some time for your own shopping: "Just let me go into this one last shop, and then we'll go see the...."

Galleries

Pioneer Square is the hub of gallery activity in Seattle. If you want to explore the galleries with your child, avoid the First Thursday of each month, for this is when new exhibits open—and stay open into the evening, attracting throngs of the Black Turtleneck People. Don't feel intimidated, however, to go during the week, just be sure to keep the following recommendations in mind.

The first, of course, is to use common sense. You know your child best, so it follows that you best know what your child is capable or incapable of doing. For instance, if your three-year-old has recently discovered the joy of throwing dishes, don't take him to a Dale Chihuly exhibit. In broader terms, if your child does not respond to the words "don't touch," then he is not ready for the gallery experience, unless you want to start an expensive collection of damaged art. Best to teach your child to regard the entire gallery as a piece of art. That means no hands on the walls and no climbing around on ledges or stairs.

Second, if you have more than one child in the two-to-eight range, arrange to take only one.

Third, don't take your child to more galleries than his creative intellect can swallow. Choose a weekday, or weekend day, when the galleries aren't apt to be too crowded, and go through two or three. There are a lot of shops in between galleries that have fun, bright windows to peer into, and several areas to share a snack and discuss what you've seen.

Finally, realize that most of the gallery owners in Pioneer Square agree that "well-behaved" children are welcome guests and that part of a gallery's function is educational. Here are just a handful of recommended galleries. Check the local paper for reviews of actual exhibits after the first of each month.

Animation U.S.A.
104 1st Ave S
625-0347
Hours: Mon-Sat, 10 am-6 pm; Sun, 12-6 pm

This is a small gallery that sells comic strip stats and cartoon 'cels' from all the major animation studios, including Hanna Barbera, Disney and Warner Bros. Though the bright colors and familiar characters will surely enchant your child, the price tags will keep your feet grounded deep in reality.

Davidson Galleries
313 Occidental Ave S
624-7684
Hours: Mon-Sat, 11 am-5:30 pm; Sun, 1-5 pm

Entering its twentieth year of exhibiting contemporary paintings, sculpture and drawings, this gallery is worth celebrating. Creaky old floorboards and a high ceiling give the space an earthy but open atmosphere. The older child might enjoy the Print Center upstairs as well.

Linda Farris Gallery
320 2nd Ave S
623-1110
Hours: Tues-Sat, 11:30 am-5 pm; Sun, 1-5 pm

The design of this gallery is in and of itself artful, with its cracked, worn tile floor and its maze of show rooms.

Flury & Company
322 1st Ave S
587-0260
Hours: Mon-Sat, 10 am-6 pm; Sun, 12-5 pm

This spacious gallery exhibits an outstanding collection of Edward S. Curtis' Native American goldtones and photographs, as well as Native American arts and crafts.

Foster/White Gallery

311 1/2 Occidental Ave S
622-2833
Hours: Mon-Sat, 10 am-5:30 pm; Sun, 12-5 pm

One of the oldest and best known galleries in the area, Foster/White represents some of the who's who of Northwest artists, including Mark Tobey, Dale Chihuly, Morris Graves and George Tsutakawa. Paintings, sculptures, ceramics and glass by lesser known contemporary artists are also featured. Don't bring any young children into this gallery; the layout is complicated and the art is everywhere.

Glasshouse Studio and Gallery

311 Occidental
682-9939
Hours: open daily, 10 am-5 pm

Though this may seem like the last place you'd want to venture into with your kids, Glasshouse Studio and Gallery is one of the more kid-friendly galleries in this area. Kids are invited to watch the glassblowers in action from 10-11 am and 11:30 am-2 pm daily. (On really hot days, they're known to stop a little earlier; on Saturdays they work a bit later.) The staff will always take the time to answer any questions, and occasionally the glassblowers themselves will take a break to talk with visitors. If you want to visit with a small group (no more than 15 kids at a time), call ahead to schedule an appointment.

Linda Hodges Gallery

410 Occidental Ave S
624-3034
Hours: Tues-Sat, 11 am-5 pm; Sun, 1-5 pm.

A particularly appealing gallery, because it is small and uncluttered. Hodges hangs artwork fairly low on the wall, which makes it much more accessible for young and old.

Greg Kucera Gallery

608 2nd Ave
624-0770
Hours: Tues-Sat, 10:30 am-5:30 pm; Sun, 1-5 pm

This young gallery, with its long narrow exhibition hall (not good for young sprinters or sculpture-bowlers), has been associated with the "we're not afraid of art" attitude since its show TABOO, which explored controversial artists and works. Though that show would not have been appropriate for most children, the gallery on the whole features contemporary painters and sculptors well worth discovering.

Mia Gallery

536 1st Ave S
467-8283
Hours: Tues-Sat, 11 am-5:30 pm; Sun, 1-5 pm

The Mia is never short on inspiring exhibits. Although shows vary greatly, all challenge ordinary perceptions of art.

Shops

The Elliott Bay Book Company

1st Ave S & S Main
624-6600
Hours: Mon-Sat, 10 am-11 pm; Sun, 12-6 pm

Elliott Bay is a favorite bookstore among local literary buffs. It now boasts a new, larger kids book section, complete with a two-story castle where kids can relax and read their selections. Elliott Bay also has a good storytelling program for children; call for the latest schedule. Downstairs is a gourmet cafe/deli with delectables such as scones, muffins, salads and sandwiches.

Grand Central Shops on the Park

214 1st Ave S

This two-story complex houses a few shops and restaurants, as well as a lovely enclosed arcade with a fireplace and scattered tables. A couple shops on the lower level are worth a visit.

The Blacksmith Shop

Grand Central/214 1st Ave S
623-4085
Hours: open daily, 11 am-5 pm

The big draw to this shop is not the merchandise, but the blacksmith. Kids can watch him work through any one of the windows in and around the shop.

Koala Australian Gift Shoppe

Grand Central/214 1st Ave S
343-0104
Hours vary

If you have one of those six- to ten-year-olds that loves collecting cutsie clutter, this shop shouldn't be missed (or should be avoided, depending on who's controlling the piggy bank).

Paper Cat
Paper Cat/Rubber Stamps

Grand Central/214 1st S
623-3636
Hours: Mon-Sat, 9 am-6:30 pm; Sun, 11 am-5 pm

If your child collects stickers or stamps, don't miss the Paper Cat and its Rubber Stamp off-shoot. The Paper Cat also features stationery, address books, cards and wrapping paper—one of the best assortments in town.

Great Winds Kite Shop

402 Occidental S
624-6886
Hours: Mon-Sat, 10 am-5:30 pm; Sun, 12-5:30 pm

Kite flying is serious business in Seattle. Perhaps people got tired of looking up only to see gray skies—they wanted to see some color and light. For whatever reason, kites are popular possessions, and this store has a good selection of them, big and small, simple and elaborate.

Magic Mouse Toys

603 1st Ave (1st & Yesler)
682-8097
Summer hours: Mon-Sat, 10 am-9 pm; Sun, 10 am-6 pm
Regular hours: Mon-Thurs, 10 am-6 pm; Fri & Sat, 10 am-9 pm; Sun, 10 am-6 pm

Though you won't find the mass-produced toys such as Fisher Price or Milton Bradley here, you will find a wide assortment of quality puzzles, art supplies, games and toys from Europe and other places around the world. Also, a very good, often missed, book selection is tucked downstairs in the back of the store. The staff is knowledgeable and amicable; kids are welcome and encouraged to do what comes naturally: play!

Ruby Montana's Pinto Pony

603 2nd Ave
Hours: open daily, 10 am-6 pm

Don't moan and groan if your child begs to take a look inside this wacky store. You'll likely be the one who just wants to stay "one more minute," when she is ready to leave. Ruby Montana's sells some of the best knickknacks in town—for kids and adults—including small toys, funky gadgets, 1950s kitsch items, and antique salt and pepper shakers.

The Seattle Sport

111 1st Ave S
624-9569
Hours: Mon-Sat, 10 am-6 pm; Sun, 11 am-5 pm

If your child's favorite landmark in Pioneer Square is the Kingdome, chances are good that the Seattle Sport will be her favorite store. Any sports fan will be impressed by the wide selection of team t-shirts, hats and related items.

Snacks/Restaurants

Bagel Express

205 1st S
682-7202
Hours: Mon-Fri, 7 am-6 pm; Sat, 11 am-5 pm

Low-priced, good bagels, starting at $1.35. Also on the menu are salads, soups and fruit.

Walter's Waffles

106 James St
382-2692
Hours: Mon-Fri, 7:30 am-5:30 pm; Sat, 10 am-4 pm

Walter's motto is "Serious Snack Waffles, Hot to Go." He should add the words "delicious" and "inexpensive" to his description. The basic snack waffle is $1.25; yummy toasted sandwiches (served on Sicilian Focaccia bread) begin at $3.75.

International District

Between 5th Ave S and 12 Ave S; S Dearborn St to W Washington St

Depending on whom you ask, this neighborhood is also known as Chinatown/International District. Whatever the politically correct term may be, you and your family will find shops, businesses and restaurants of all Asian persuasions—Chinese, Japanese, Korean, Filipino, Thai and others—in this dilapidated but spirited section of town.

The International District is difficult to describe beyond the cultures it represents. Though its boundaries are somewhat defined, there is no grand pegoda to say you've arrived, no tourist strip that contains all the must-see shops and sights, and no 24-hour bustling crowd. Instead, it is a scattered, undeveloped treasure of Seattle, with some sparkling highlights and an overwhelming amount of potential. Make sure to point out the detail on the street lamps and phone booths to your children, and plan on holding up the younger ones so that they can see some of the more lively store windows—especially along the north side of S King St, where they'll come face to glass with large fish, roasted delicacies, and other colorful spectacles. Note also some of the colorful portals and balconies along 7th Ave S.

☆ Essentials

Though you can drive to and park in the International District without too much hassle, it is also accessible by bus and by trolley (which comes up from the waterfront and Pioneer Square). You can't miss the International District bus station's teal, purple and pink decor on S King and 5th Ave S. The Waterfront Streetcar stop is at S Jackson on 5th Ave S.

☆ Tips

One of the best times to visit the International District is on Saturday morning, when the locals are doing their shopping, and the International Market is set up along 5th Ave S and S King St, at the entrance to the Metro Tunnel. You can explore it any other day of the week as well, but you won't get as good of a sense of its atmosphere and diversity. What we don't recommend is going on a leisurely tour in the early evening or nighttime hours, because it is fairly desolate and can be intimidating. This shouldn't stop you from taking the kids to one of its many great restaurants for dinner.

Highlights

Chinatown Discovery Tours

419 7th Ave S
236-0657

The Chinatown Discovery Tours were started by a prominent woman in the Chinese community named Vi Mar to educate people as to the value of the International District and to promote understanding, acceptance and support of the city's Asian community. She offers several different tour packages, including a one-and-a-half-hour "mo chann" (no food) tour, a three-and-a-half hour lunch tour, and a tea tour, all of which can be catered to youth or family groups.

With 122 nieces and nephews, and three children of her own, Vi is no stranger to children, and she'll spend the first part of the tour (which is spent in the office) getting the kids' minds in motion—asking pointed questions and engaging them with stories of her own experiences as a Chinese woman born and raised in the area. Everyone will enjoy Vi's charming husband, Howard, who steps out of his role at the registration desk to teach everyone how to use the Chinese abacus (a manual calculator that uses wooden beads).

Though the walking part of the tour is short, Vi does state that she will cater the tour to cover whatever interests the group—so be sure to state your expectations up front, especially if you wish to spend more time exploring the area.

Danny Woo International District Community Garden

S Main & Maynard Ave S

This terraced community garden, located below Kobe Terrace Park, is worth walking through if you are heading up Maynard to see the Kobe lantern. Though it is not a spectacular sight in and of itself, it does exhibit a certain charm with its windy cobblestone and gravel paths, and small produce gardens.

Hing Hay Park

S King & Maynard Ave S

Marked by a red and orange ornate pavilion, which was donated by the Taiwan government, Hing Hay Park is a central gathering place for people—and pigeons. Hing Hay means "good fortune" in Chinese, and maybe if your family has a seat on one of the many benches in this red-bricked park, some of the luck will rub off on you.

International Children's Park

S Lane St & 7th Ave S

If you are exploring the area with toddlers, take them to this little park for a break. The park, which is primarily a big sandbox, features a winding slide, a patch of grass, some big climbing rocks and a dragon sculpture kids can sit on (with a little help). Parents will appreciate the abundant benches. Don't bother heading further south of this park if on foot.

Kobe Terrace Park

S Main & Maynard Ave S; accessible from S Washington as well

In 1976, Seattle's Japanese sister

city, Kobe, gave the International District a stone lantern, with the stated hope that it would "shed light on the friendship between the peoples of Kobe and Seattle forever." The cement lantern, which sits upon a bed of rocks, is not going to make your kids jump up and down with excitement, but the walk through the park and the Danny Woo Community Garden below is entertaining enough.

Tsutakawa Sculpture

Maynard Ave S, just below S Jackson St

Renowned Northwest artist, George Tsutakawa, built this abstract, tree-like sculpture, as the central feature of what was to be a fountain. Instead, however, the funds for this project dried up, so it was finished as you see it now—grounded in a cement pot, thirstier than ever.

Wall Mural

S King & Maynard Ave S

Up on a brick wall that flanks the north side of Hing Hay Park, this colorful mural tells the history of Asians in Seattle, from their early efforts in building the railroads to their modern day involvement in the community. The kids will notice the primary figure in the mural is a dragon—a powerful but good symbol in this piece.

Wing Luke Museum

407 7th Ave S
623-5124
Hours: Tues-Fri, 11 am-4:30 pm; Sat-Sun, 12-4 pm
Admission: $2.50/adults; $1.50/ seniors & students; $.75/children 5-12 years
Annual membership: $50/family

The Wing Luke Asian Museum, showcases the many artistic contributions of Seattle's Asian cultures and the diversities among them. Part of the museum is devoted to teaching people about the hardship and discrimination Asians have suffered here—an important and sometimes forgotten history that kids should learn. (See Kid Culture/Exhibits & Museums).

Shops

Uwajimaya

519 6th Ave S
624-6248
Hours: daily, 9 am-8 pm (extended to 9 pm in the summer)
Free one-hour parking in lot

Even if you're not out of canned bananas, dried fish or Thai chilies, Uwajimaya is an irresistible stop in the International District. Whether you take your kids down the food aisles to show them the culinary delights of Japan, China, Korea or the Philippines, or take them upstairs to see the colorful assortment of dolls, stationery and textiles, this place is sure to capture their curiosity.

A trip to Uwajimaya is never

complete without examining some of the less familiar fruits and vegetables, visiting the live geoduck, crab and clam tank, sampling the fresh sushi (or at least watching the sushi chefs in action) and browsing through the book area. The books and magazines, sold on the upper level of the store, have an amazing visual appeal, with most titles in elegant characters instead of English letters, and covers that open on the left instead of the right.

As you walk around, notice the packaging and labels on soda, candies and toys (three things bound to appeal to the kids, though the American baseball card vending machine will likely be a great hit, too), and treat everyone to a box of rice candy as you leave—they won't believe they can eat the wrapping!

Snacks/Restaurants

With over seven bakeries and over 60 restaurants, the International District is not short on snack spots. Although many Seattleites have their favorites, each place has a different charm and appeal (some even have photos of their dishes in the window). Be adventurous and try something new—have a Dim Sum brunch, or head to a sushi bar—you'll learn more about the area by testing what each culture has to offer.

Green Village
721 S King St
624-3634
Green Village 2
514 6th Ave S
621-1719

See Basics/Restaurants.

The Seattle Center

No child would pass up a visit to the Seattle Center: Any place that maintains a carnival atmosphere is bound to be a hit. But this 74-acre area on lower Queen Anne is not just an amusement park with dizzying rides and garish frills, it is a place where families can see first-rate children's theatre productions, get into some hands-on science experiments and art projects, sample foods from all over the world, and roll and tumble on soft green lawns.

Constructed for the 1962 World's Fair, the Seattle Center has continued to host events, celebrations and festivals to bring the community together. Its vast expanse offers a multitude of indoor and outdoor activities and encompasses various fine arts and sports facilities. Some of its better known residents are the Seattle Symphony, the Seattle Opera, the Seattle SuperSonics and the Seattle Repertory Theatre, as well as some of this city's finest family-oriented institutions that have been identified throughout this book.

☆ *Essentials*

You can expect to pay for parking around the Seattle Center, and there may be tedious traffic if there is an event happening. Fortunately, parking lots are plentiful, except on the south side.

If you are heading to the center from the downtown area, opt for taking the Monorail (684-7200) from Westlake Center—the ride is just under two minutes, and it will land you smack in the middle of the Center's action. Kids five and under ride free on the Monorail; one-way fares are $.80/adults, $.60/children ages 5-12 and $.25/seniors and disabled persons. The Monorail runs about every 15 minutes (more often around lunch time), and can be accessed from the third floor of the Westlake Mall or in the Seattle Center's Fun Forest (these are its only stops). Winter hours: Sun-Thurs, 9 am-9 pm; Fri-Sat, 9 am-

☆ *Tips*

Going to the Seattle Center for the entire day to "do it all" would not only transform your sweet little angels into snarling brats, but it would likely deplete their college funds. With so much to do at the Center, you are better off deciding as a family which appeals to you most (i.e., the Fun Forest or the Pacific Science Center) and then seeing where you stand—or if you stand—at the end of that activity.

midnight. Summer hours (mid-June through Labor Day): daily, 9 am-midnight.

Highlights

The Charlotte Martin Theatre

443-0807; ticket office, 633-4567
Season runs October through May
Ticket price: $8.50/children; $14.50/ adults

Rated one of the top children's theatre companies in the United States, the Seattle Children's Theatre will be performing at this new Center facility starting in September of 1993. In addition to its season of theatre productions, the Education Department of Seattle Children's Theatre offers a full array of performing arts classes and workshops for children, teens and adults, as well as outreach programs, programs for teachers, school residency programs and the Young Actors Institute, all designed to teach and encourage participation in the performing arts. See Kid Culture/Theatres for details.

Children's Museum

Seattle Center House, lower level
441-1768
Hours: Tues-Sun, 10 am-5 pm; open daily during the summer months
Admission: $3.50/person; children under 12 months are free
Annual membership: $35/family

The Children's Museum offers the best in creative, interactive play for young children in the city. The crux of this museum is a child-sized neighborhood, where kids can move from establishment to establishment and role-play. See Kid Culture/Exhibits & Museums.

Pacific Arts Center

443-5437
Hours: Tues-Sat, 10 am-4 pm
Nominal admission; donations appreciated
Annual membership: $25/family

Pacific Arts Center began as a volunteer program in the 1940s, bringing storytelling and arts experiences to children in the Seattle area. It was later moved to the Seattle Center grounds, and has been undergoing renovations. Scheduled to open in August 1993, the refurbished facility will host a full array of classes and workshops in all artistic disciplines. See Kid Culture/Exhibits & Museums.

Pacific Science Center

443-2001
Hours: Mon-Fri, 10 am-5 pm; Sat, Sun and holidays, 10 am-6 pm
Admission: $6.50/adults; $5.50/ children 6-13 years & seniors; $4.50/ children 2-5 years.
Annual membership: $35/family

At Pacific Science Center kids can go from exhibit to exhibit, testing their eyesight, weight, strength and eating habits; experimenting with different musical instruments, bubbles, mirrors and

Photo credit: Paul Dowling

Arches at the Pacific Science Center.

gravity; and discovering why the world is the place it is. An ideal destination for any age child, it is a veritable science playground. See Kid Culture/Exhibits & Museums.

Fun Forest

728-1585
Hours: open daily June 1-Labor Day, noon to midnight; limited weekend operation remainder of year
Prices: 1 ticket/$.85; book of 8/ $5.50; book of 18/$11

The Seattle Center's aforementioned carnival atmosphere—complete with the requisite sights, sounds and smells—is captured in an area at the foot of the Space Needle called the Fun Forest. Before you enter its confines however, be sure to prepare your child for the mighty temptations of giant stuffed bears, clouds of cotton candy and rides that are over much too quickly. Negotiate the terms of the outing—type of snacks, number of rides—so you won't have to be the cruel fun squasher when you get asked for more of everything.

On the south side of the Fun Forest, toddlers and preschoolers can find their pint-sized thrills on the merry-go-round, antique autos, boats, etc., while you send their more daring brothers and sisters over to try out the Orbiter, Galion, Wild River and—if they are really at a brush-with-death stage—the new Windstorm Roller Coaster that opened in June of 1993.

Tickets can be purchased individually or at a discounted rate in books of eight and 18. Discount book tickets can be used throughout the Fun Forest season.

Skate Boarding Park

6th Ave N at Republican, east of main Center grounds

At press time, it was difficult to get an answer as to when this park was due to open and what it would entail. The only information known is this: It will open sometime in the summer of 1993 as a cushioned open-air facility and will later be a covered complex, offering skateboarding classes and programs, as well as hosting competitions. Call the general information number at the Seattle Center if you would like more information.

Space Needle

Ticket prices (for elevator ride to Observation Deck): $6/adults; $5/seniors; $4/children 5-11 years; children under 5 are free
Group rates are also available

There must be some unwritten rule stating that any city that hosts a world fair must gather its finest architects and engineers, make them watch a week of *The Jetsons*, and then have them construct some space-inspired, Astro Period landmark. If so, the Space Needle was built by the books. Now, over 30 years later, the Needle still looks impressively futuristic, though its once staggering height (605 feet in all) has since been dwarfed by downtown buildings.

Yet, the Space Needle remains one of the best vantage points in Seattle. Visitors can take one of the elevators (nicknamed "beetles" because of their color and design) up 518 feet, to the Observation Deck, for a panoramic view of the city, the Olympic and Cascade mountains, Puget Sound and Mount Rainier. The Needle also features two revolving restaurants at the 500-foot level (one full rotation every hour), but some don't think the thrill is worth the price for family dining.

Snacks/Restaurants

The Center grounds are littered with concession stands, selling all the usual treats for exorbitant prices. If the kids are up for a more filling (though not necessarily healthier) snack, brace yourself and head to the Food Circus at the Center House. What you'll see is restaurant after restaurant, lined up. And, unless you pay close attention, the next thing you'll notice is that your entire family has suddenly dispersed, each heading in search of the most palatable meal (and none heading in the same direction). Be prepared to stand in a few lines before everyone is happy.

CHAPTER 9

Out-of-Town Excursions

Seattle neighborhoods have become so self-sufficient and contained that you rarely need to travel beyond your own community to find a decent park, a good book or video shop, and life's little necessities. Handy as it may seem, your easy living may be eroding your sense of adventure and limiting your child's "real life" perspective.

When you realize that the quality time that you've been spending with the kids has become routine or predictable, then it's time to blow out of town—at least for a few hours. Hop on a train for a day trip to Tacoma, go to Olympia and see our legislators in action, visit a nearby city's children's museum, take a ride on an authentic steamboat. You won't need suitcases or motel reservations for these activities, and everyone will benefit from the total change of scenery.

Boeing Tour Center

Boeing Everett Plant, Exit 189 from I-5
(206)342-4801
Public tours, Mon-Fri, 9 am, 10 am, 11 am, 1 pm, 2 pm & 3 pm
Free

Free tours of Boeing's Everett Plant are offered for ages 10 and up on weekdays on a first-come, first-served basis. It begins with a half-hour video presentation in the plant's theatre, and continues at a moderate pace through the factory, covering about one-third of a mile in all, including some steep stairs. The tour ends with a drive along the flight line. No photographic equipment is permitted. Group tours for 10 or more visitors are offered on weekdays between the hours of 8:30 am and 10:30 am by reservation only. The lobby and gift shop are open Monday-Friday, 8:30 am-4 pm.

☆ Tips

Summer tours at the Boeing Tour Center are very popular, so plan on arriving at least one hour prior to desired tour time, and don't be surprised if you end up waiting longer. The 9 am and 1 pm tours accommodate up to 90 people (others are limited to 45).

Capitol Tours

State Capitol, Olympia
During session (odd years from Jan-Apr; even years, Jan-Mar):
House of Representatives, (206)786-7773 or Senate, (206) 786-7703
Between sessions: (206)586-8687
Tours offered daily on the hour starting at 10 am; last tour at 3 pm
For State Capitol Museum Tours call (206)753-1998
Free

The more a parent knows about the workings and wonders of government, the more difficult it seems to explain to kids—to just give the nuts and bolts of the system (how it is supposed to work) without getting into the complexities of donkeys and elephants and all the muddling issues and scandals (why it doesn't always work). Taking your children on a docent-led tour of the State Capitol will get you off the hook and back to good old terms like "bicameral" and "filibuster."

During the legislative session, tours include a visit to Senate and House chambers whenever possible, for a close-up view of Washington's elected officials in action. Tours during this time tend to be very crowded; reservations are suggested.

Specialty tours of the Legislative, Judicial and Executive branches, as well as of the Governor's Mansion, the State Capitol Museum and historical landmarks can be arranged. These tours most often run two to four hours in length and can be tailored to any visitors, from

> ☆ ***Tips***
>
> *On your trip to the Capitol, bring a lunch and enjoy a picnic on the beautiful Capitol and conservatory grounds. Young people ages 10 and up are eligible to go on the Dome Tour—bring good walking shoes as the trip includes 262 stairs to the top of the Dome. Everyone under age 21 must be accompanied by an adult.*
>
> *The Governor's Mansion is also open for tours on Wednesday afternoons by reservation only; no children's groups under sixth grade level will be admitted.*

preschoolers to adults, physically and mentally challenged persons, school groups or individuals. Reservations for specialty tours are required.

☆ *Essentials*

Between sessions, parking is available just outside the Capitol building for $.50/hour. (Bring your quarters!) During the session, parking is available in designated Visitor Center Parking areas only.

The Children's Museum Northwest

227 Prospect, Bellingham
(206)733-8769
Hours: Tues-Wed, 12-5 pm; Thurs-Sat, 10 am-5 pm; Sun, 12-5 pm
Admission: $2/person

The Children's Museum Northwest, located in downtown Bellingham, offers hands-on fun for children from toddler age to about eight years. Current expansion will create new exhibits, designed to entertain children up to about 12 years of age.

Children's Museum of Tacoma

925 Court C, Tacoma
(206)627-2436
Hours: Tues-Fri, 10 am-5 pm; Saturday, 10 am-4 pm; Sunday, 12-4 pm
Admission: $3.50/person

The Children's Museum of Tacoma devotes much of its space to a major thematic exhibit, which changes every 18 months. Specific programs, workshops and hands-on activities are designed in conjunction with the exhibit's theme to enhance a child's creativity, comprehension and learning. The current exhibit, Buildings, will be on display until June 1994, introducing children to the world of architecture by exploring its history, elements and technology. Though these exhibits are primarily tailored for elementary age children, older and younger siblings will likely find something that strikes their interests as well.

Permanent exhibits at the Children's Museum of Tacoma include a child-sized street, complete with a cafe, post office and bank to visit. Groups are always welcome; call in advance for reservations.

Creation Station

7505 Olympic View Dr, Edmonds
775-7959
Hours: Tues & Thurs, 11 am-7 pm; Mon, Wed, Fri & Sat, 11 am-4 pm
Cost: $2/child per project; $1-$8/take-home bag of materials

As any parent knows, the stuff that we consider "junk" is often, in the eyes of a child, the material for creation. C.C. Leonard, owner of the Creation Station agrees. "I hate to see anything thrown away," she says, which explains why she was inspired to open a store where kids (and adults) can pick and choose from 160 barrels filled with assorted gadgets and materials. Leonard is a born recycler, and a scavenger for the stuff that local businesses consider rubbish.

The store is chock full of unusual and unused, uncontaminated, recyclable materials such as cones, tubes, fabrics, plastic, paper, foam, containers and wood. Expert guidance is available, complete with lots of ideas on how to use the various materials (although Leonard, a former preschool teacher, is quick to point out kids don't need any help with ideas.)

Creation Station has tables set up with loads of material to spur creativity, accommodating up to 30 children at a time. If your children would rather work at home, however, they may fill a bag with whatever materials they choose from the enormous selection ($1-$8).

Enchanted Village & Wild Waves Water Park

36201 Enchanted Pkwy S, Federal Way
661-8001
Hours: open mid-April through Labor Day; seasonal hours vary
Admission: Enchanted Village only, $7.50-$9.50; Wild Waves & Enchanted Village combination, $12.50-$18
Season passes: $59.95-$79.95

Pack a picnic and spend the day enjoying 50 acres of family fun and excitement at Wild Waves Water Park and Enchanted Village in Federal Way. The price of admission will feel steep so plan on getting there early and spending time at both Wild Waves and Enchanted Village in order to get your money's worth.

Enchanted Village is a magical place for young children. It is a quiet, forested setting—a pleasant switch from the carnival atmosphere inherent to most amusement parks. It offers several activities likely to drive any kid to delirium, including 14 amusement rides, wading pools, bumper boats, the Antique Doll and Toy Museum, the Wax Museum, the Amazing Maze and the 13-hole Krogolf Course (a small version of putt-putt golf). Admission to Enchanted Village includes unlimited use of rides and other attractions, including live entertainment, puppet shows and magic shows; there are additional fees for arcade games, video games, remote controlled boats and clown face painting.

Wild Waves is the Northwest's largest water park—20 acres of water mania including giant waterslides and a 24,000-square-foot wave pool. There are a few smaller slides and water rides for the younger set, but this park is most popular with ages eight and up. The giant water slides are best reserved for older children and adults.

Admission to Wild Waves always includes admission to Enchanted Village. Birthday parties, company picnics and other kinds of group events are welcome and receive discounted admission.

☆ Essentials

There is no admission to Wild Waves only. Food concessions, raft rentals, video games and lockers are also available for additional fees. Parking costs $2 per day.

☆ Tips

Though this may be an expensive outing for parents, we haven't met a child yet (including teenagers) who doesn't consider it a favorite destination. It works well to arrive around 10 or 11 am, have a picnic at lunch time, and then leave about a half hour before the park closes, to avoid the traffic jam right at closing time. There are several fast food places (Dairy Queen, McDonald's, etc.) in Federal Way, where you can get dinner before you get back on the freeway. Food is not allowed in the Wild Waves area (very strictly enforced), but Enchanted Village, which is a short, easy walk from Wild Waves, sells food and has many pleasant picnic areas.

As could be expected, the crowds are enormous at Wild Waves on hot summer days, especially on weekends (Saturday is busiest). Expect long lines for everything except the water park for very young children, where toddlers and preschoolers can come and go without waiting.

Enchanted Village and Wild Waves are well supervised. The staff is helpful and courteous; the rides and facilities are exceptionally clean and well maintained.

Pioneer Farm Museum

7716 Ohop Valley Rd, Eatonville (south of Puyallup)
(206) 832-6300
Hours: seasonal hours vary; closed Thanksgiving through February
$4-$5; children 2 & under free

After the long (about one and a half hours) ride from Seattle, you and your kids might be disappointed when you first see the sparsc, drab setting of Pioneer Farm. The owners of this farm have aimed to give an authentic (not Disney) depiction of life in pioneer times. Once the one-and-a-half hour tour begins, however, most school-age children will be enthralled to learn how people lived 100 years ago. The tour includes a visit to a log cabin, barn, blacksmith and wood shop and allows children to participate in more than 100 activities, such as scrubbing clothes, sawing wood, carding wool, grinding wheat and milking the cow.

☆ Tips

The Pioneer Farm is not a pristine museum tour but a hands-on experience where participants get down and dirty, so dress accordingly.

Pioneer Farm also offers a variety of programs for school and private groups that explore the Native American culture and pioneer heritage. These programs include storytelling, participatory activities, history, Indian lore and environmental history of the region. Groups may also register for an overnight adventure, in which they extend their pioneering activities into the night—cooking over an open fire and sleeping in the hayloft.

Ste. Michelle Winery

14111 NE 145th, Woodinville
488-1133
Hours: open year-round Mon, 10 am-4:30 pm & Tues-Sun, 10 am-6 pm
Admission & tours are free

The award-winning Ste. Michelle Winery presents a variety of activities throughout the year, in addition to its own cellar tours and wine tastings, which occur daily. Though your children won't be able to participate in the tasting, they are allowed to take the tour, which lasts about 45 minutes and is free of charge. Cellar tours leave the lobby about every half hour and are stroller/ wheelchair accessible. Groups are welcome.

During the spring and summer months, the grounds of Ste. Michelle are host to a vast assortment of entertainment, including jazz, classical and contemporary music concerts, theatre presentations and dance performances. Many of these events are free, and the public is invited to bring a picnic, spread out on the lawn, and enjoy the entertainment, which has included such performers as the Bellevue Philharmonic Orchestra and Pacific Northwest Ballet. For a complete schedule of summertime events, call 488-3300.

Sea-Tac International Airport

Parking: $2/two hours (first half hour free)

Ever notice that when a two-year-old goes to Disneyland, the subway train ride on the way to the plane is the highlight of the trip? Instead of pulling your child through the airport on a quick dash to the plane, make Sea-Tac the final destination for a novel and inexpensive outing.

☆ *Tips*

Ste. Michelle Winery is a good turn-around point for families riding the Sammamish River bike trail from Marymoor Park in Redmond. (See Biking in Active Play: Outdoor Fun for more information.) There is a short strip of busy road between the trail and the winery where young riders should walk their bikes, but otherwise it's fairly safe.

Don't miss the winery's excellent gift shop—the Wine Shop—which sells picnic items, gourmet foods and wine accessories.

The terminals for Horizon Air, one of the smaller, locally based airlines, offer a first-rate opportunity to observe the entire travel process from landing to take off. Watch the planes being fueled and loaded with luggage and the passengers boarding and disembarking from the planes. Wander through the gift shops, check out the abundant art, witness a few tearful greetings and good-byes and then head back home for lunch and a nap—just the right amount of travel and adventure for a preschooler.

Snohomish River Queen

1712 W Marine View Dr, Everett
(206)259-2743
Operates year-round; six days per week throughout summer
Ticket prices: $15.95-$29.95; children 12 & under are half price

The Snohomish River Queen, a modern replica paddlewheel steamboat, leaves the Everett Marina for narrated tours of the marina and Snohomish River Wetlands. The double-deck steamboat offers views of the Olympic Mountains, Jetty Island and the passing river scenery. Inside, passengers will find information, pictures and photographs illustrating Everett's history and the early riverboats on Puget Sound; a player piano entertains along the way.

Historic River and Scenic Wildlife tours are offered, as well as lunch, Sunday brunch and dinner cruises. Special event cruises include Mother's Day, Easter and Christmas. Reservations are required.

Snoqualmie Falls Park

Located 25 miles east of Seattle; take exit 27 from I-90
Open year-round
Free admission

This scenic park, located in the foothills of the Cascade Mountains, is a fine place to give your kids a good view of a waterfall (go in late spring or early summer when the snow is melting). Just outside the town of Snoqualmie, the Snoqualmie River plunges (some say this is an overstatement) 270 feet over a rock gorge. Puget Power owns and operates the two-acre park, as well as the Snoqualmie Falls Hydroelectric Project, which has been generating electricity since 1898.

The park's grounds feature observation platforms to view the falls, picnic areas, restrooms, a gift shop and cafe. For the ambitious, the half-mile River Trail leads down to the river's edge, for a spectacular view of the cascading falls. The trail is steep, however, so be prepared to help the little ones on the trip back up.

Tacoma Art Museum

1123 Pacific Ave, Tacoma
(206)272-4258
Hours: Tues-Sat, 10 am-5 pm; Sun, 12-5 pm
Admission: $2-$3/per person; admission is free on Tuesdays

A special feature of the Tacoma Art Museum is ArtWORKS, a workspace devoted to hands-on activities for the entire family. The activities explore the themes presented in the current exhibits being showcased in the museum's main galleries. Admission to ArtWORKS is included in museum admission.

Train Rides

A train ride is one of the best outings you can take with your child. The immensity of the engine, the commotion and flurry of departure and the soothing motion once underway never fail to fascinate children (and most adults). On your short journey you can sit back and have a real visit—leaving behind the stress and strain of everyday life. Bring snacks and books if you think your fellow traveler might get restless.

Amtrak

Stations:
3rd Ave at S Jackson, Seattle
1001 Puyallup Ave, Tacoma
800-872-7245
Ticket prices: round trip $12/adult; $6/children

A day trip on Amtrak will give your child the thrill of a ride on a real choo-choo, without the hassle of overnight travel. Tacoma is a perfect destination—the ride lasts just about as long as your child's attention span, ensuring that the trip home will be eagerly anticipated, not dreaded. Spend the bulk of the day exploring Tacoma's many attractions, including Point Defiance Zoo & Aquarium (see the Animals, Animals, Animals chapter). Plan it so that you jump back on board just as your stomachs are beginning to rumble and have dinner chez Amtrak.You'll get the kids home just in time for bed.

Trains depart from Seattle at 7:30 am and 9:50 am daily, arriving in Tacoma at 8:24 am and 10:47 am respectively.

For the return trip, trains depart from Tacoma at 5:06 pm and 6:53 pm, arriving in Seattle at 6:10 pm and 8:05 pm respectively.

Reservations are strongly recommended.

Lake Whatcom Railway

Located 10 miles north of Sedro Woolley on State Highway 9, about 2 hours from Seattle in Wickersham
PO Box 91, Acme, WA 98220
(206) 595-2218
Special excursions year-round; call for complete schedule
Ticket prices: $10/adults; $5/children; rates vary for special events

Throughout the year, the Lake Whatcom Railway offers scenic tours of Whatcom County aboard coaches pulled by an authentic steam engine #1070, built in 1907. Passengers travel along seven miles of the Northern Pacific railway, built in 1903, on a one-and-a-quarter hour journey through forest land, breathtaking scenery and a tunnel (always a highlight). Special excursions, complete with entertainment, refreshments and appearances by special characters, occur on Valentines Day, St. Patrick's Day, Easter, Father's Day and Independence Day, and in autumn and December (the Santa Train). In addition, the train runs twice daily every Saturday and Tuesday, mid-June through August. Reservations are required as space is limited; send a self-addressed stamped envelope to the above address for tickets.

Mt. Rainier Scenic Railroad

Located about 40 miles south of Tacoma on Hwy 7 in Elbe
569-2588
Scenic Railroad Schedule: departs three times per day, weekends, Memorial Day through the end of Sept; daily, mid-June through Labor Day
Ticket prices: $6.95/adults; $5.95/seniors; $4.95/juniors, 12-17 years; $3.95/children under 12

Mt. Rainier Scenic Railroad's vintage steam locomotives depart Elbe for hour-and-a-half steam train excursions through the foothills of Mt. Rainier, 14 miles to Mineral Lake. If the extraordinary scenery doesn't keep your kids completely absorbed, the live music surely will. No reservations are required for this ride.

If you want to give an older child a real treat, the Cascadian Dinner Train offers a complete five-course prime rib dinner during a four-hour train ride from Elbe to the logging town of Morton. The Dinner Train departs Elbe April-Memorial Day and October-November at 1 pm, on Sundays; and Memorial Day-September at 5:30 pm on Saturdays. Prepaid reservations are required; the cost is $55/person.

Puget Sound and Snoqualmie Valley Railway

PO Box 459, Snoqualmie, WA 98065
(206) 888-0373 or (206) 746-4025
Weekends only, Apr-Oct; call to confirm departure times
Ticket prices: $6/adults; $5/seniors; $4/children; children under 3 are free

Travel aboard the historic Puget Sound and Snoqualmie Valley steam train for a one-and-a-quarter hour trip through the scenic Snoqualmie Valley. The train leaves the Snoqualmie Depot, travels to North Bend, and on through the Snoqualmie Valley along the South Fork of the Snoqualmie River, over trestles and through rural areas in the shadow of Mount Si. The excursion returns along the same tracks through the town of Snoqualmie, near the famous Snoqualmie Falls. The train runs each weekend from Memorial Day through Labor Day, as well as select days during the spring and fall. No reservations are necessary.

The Railway offers two special events during the year: the Spook Train, offering young ghosts and goblins a special Halloween treat, and the popular Santa Train, complete with Old Saint Nick and lots of goodies. The Santa Train sells out long before December; call for reservations in early fall.

The Snoqualmie Railway Museum, located at the depot, is open each Friday, Saturday and Sunday when the train is running and features railroad artifacts and photographs. Admission is free.

Washington State Historical Museum

315 N Stadium Way, Tacoma
593-2830
Hours: Tues-Sat, 10 am-5 pm; Sun, 1-5 pm
Admission: $1-$2/person; $5/family groups

Explore Washington State history with a trip to the Washington State Historical Museum in Tacoma, which showcases our state's history and heritage. The ongoing exhibit, Washington: Home, Frontier, Crossroads, features over 800 artifacts as well as a multi-media presentation illustrating Washington's history. In addition, temporary exhibits illustrate specific events, places and people from the Evergreen state.

See also:
Active Play: Outdoor Fun; Animals, Animals, Animals; Harvests; and Season by Season for more ideas for out-of-town outings.

CHAPTER 10

Season by Season

Seattleites don't need blizzards, hurricanes and monsoons to tell us when a new season is upon us. We can take the family for a drive, just an hour north to show them the wonder of snow in winter. We can pack them up and drive five hours to Eastern Washington if we think they need to experience real heat in the summer. Or we can just take part in any of the many festivals or events that have come to mark the holidays or capture the spirit of spring, summer, winter and fall.

Here, you'll find a calendar of events and activities that can take the doldrums out of any month. Ride on a Santa train at Christmas time, catch a glimpse of the whales as they migrate in April, take off to a berry farm in the hot summer sun, or harvest a pumpkin for Halloween.

Photo credit: Robert Cole

For up-to-date information on these and many more special events and seasonal activities held throughout the Puget Sound area, check the monthly Calendar and Going Places listing inside *Seattle's Child*, *Eastside Parent*, or *Pierce County Parent*—Northwest Parent Publishing's newsmagazines for parents. Call 441-0191 for information on obtaining a complimentary copy or a subscription.

Winter

Model Railroad Show

Pacific Science Center, 443-2001
November

This annual event over Thanksgiving Day weekend features model train layouts, music from the railroad era, workshops and hands-on activities.

Nordic Yulefest

Nordic Heritage Museum, 789-5707
November

Celebrate the beginning of the holiday season at the annual Nordic Yulefest, which highlights the crafts, music, dance and food of Scandinavia. Kids may have their picture taken with the Nordic Santa Claus.

Celebration Especially for Children

Bellevue Art Museum, 454-3322
November-December

Each year, the Bellevue Art Museum presents a special exhibit as part of its Especially for Children Series. Designed specifically for kids, the program may also include workshops and special activities based on the subject of the exhibit.

Peter Pan

Intiman Theatre, Seattle Center, 626-0782
November-December

The Intiman Theatre received rave reviews for the 1992 inaugural run of its production of the original stage play of "Peter Pan" by J.M. Barrie and has decided to make this popular production an annual event. The production is *not* recommended for children under six years of age.

The Nutcracker

Pacific Northwest Ballet, 441-2424
North Seattle Ballet, 364-1639
Olympic Ballet Theatre in Edmonds, 774-7570
Emily's Dance Arts in Bellevue, 746-3659
November-December

Each year, Pacific Northwest Ballet performs "The Nutcracker" at the Seattle Opera House with a spectacular Maurice Sendak set. It is a dazzling production but beyond many parents' budgets. Many local dance studios and dance companies perform this holiday favorite also, often featuring young performers. These smaller-scale productions are low priced and often a great hit with young audiences.

A Christmas Carol

ACT Theatre, 285-3220; tickets 285-5110
November-December

Introduce your child to the holiday morality tale of Scrooge and Tiny Tim with this outstanding production at ACT Theatre, located on lower Queen Anne. Recommended for ages five and up. Ticket prices ranges from $12 to $23.

KING 5 Winterfest

Seattle Center, 684-7200
Late November-early January

The KING 5 winter festival features daily entertainment, ice skating on a tiny outdoor rink, arts and crafts, workshops, and loads of activities. Held each year from Thanksgiving until the first part of the New Year on the Seattle Center grounds.

Seattle Civic Christmas Ship
684-4360
Early December

The annual sailing of the Seattle Civic Christmas Ship includes stops along the shores of Lake Washington, Elliott Bay and Lake Union. Local choirs aboard the Christmas Ship and her sister vessels entertain the scores of people who gather to enjoy bonfires on the beach, colored lights on the boats and fine Christmas music.

Christmas Tree Cutting

If going to the local lot for your Christmas tree sounds too easy, venture forth to the woods with ax and family. (See Harvests/Christmas Tree Cutting.)

Christmas Tree Lighting & Bavarian Ice Fest
Leavenworth Chamber of Commerce, (509) 548-5807
December, January

The Leavenworth Chamber presents the Christmas Tree Lighting Ceremony on the first two weekends in December. The Bavarian Ice Fest is held over the Martin Luther King, Jr., holiday weekend in January and features snowshoe races, tug-of-war contests and special children's activities.

Ferry Merry Christmas
Music Center of the Northwest, 783-2798
December

The special holiday concert aboard the Seattle to Bremerton ferry held in mid-December features a small string orchestra, chorus, sing-alongs and Santa. Donations benefit Northwest Harvest.

Festival of Light
Children's Museum, 441-1768
December

The Children's Museum's annual event celebrates winter holidays from around the world and features music, hands-on activities and storytelling.

Santa Trains
December

The Lake Whatcom Railway (206-595-2218) and the Puget Sound and Snoqualmie Valley Railroad (206-888-9311) offer special Santa Trains during December. Children get to ride on these authentic steam trains, receive goodies and visit with Santa. Call early in the fall for reservations, as tickets sell quickly.

Teddy Bear Suite

Four Seasons Olympic Hotel, Seattle, 621-1700
December

Every December, the Four Seasons Olympic Hotel in downtown Seattle converts one of its rooms into a teddy bear wonderland complete with an antique bed, lots of teddy bears dressed for bedtime, a decorated Christmas tree, music, treats and a special place for parents to read from a collection of teddy bear books. A fun place to take a break on a busy shopping day. There is no charge.

Tubing and Sledding

Snow Flake Tubing and Snow Play
Snoqualmie Pass, 285-TUBE
Ski season

Snow Flake is open during the ski season at Snoqualmie Pass near Ski Acres. Rent or bring inner tubes for the kids; a rope tow will pull them up the hill. There is also a small area for sledding, but sleds are not available for rent. (See Active Play: Outdoor Fun/Tubing and Sledding.)

Voices of Christmas

Seattle Group Theatre, 441-1299
December

This popular show is designed for the entire family and features winter

Photo Credit: Carrie E. Jorgensen

The Museum of History and Industry includes hands-on activities for all ages at special holiday events.

holiday traditions from around the world in a unique theatrical revue including music, comedy, poetry and storytelling. Tickets go on sale in early September.

Zoolights

Point Defiance Zoo & Aquarium, (206) 591-5337
December

Each December, the Point Defiance Zoo & Aquarium is transformed into a fantasy land of lights. Zoolights features thousands of lights covering pathways, trees and buildings, and illuminating animals, nursery rhymes and local landmarks. Crowds are smallest in early December.

Museum of History and Industry

324-1125
December

Each year during the holidays, the Museum of History and Industry hosts a special event and/or exhibit celebrating holiday traditions with activities for the entire family.

Chanukah Celebration

Stroum Jewish Community Center, Mercer Island, 232-7115
December

A large community gathering with games, lighting of menorahs and latkes.

Science Circus

Pacific Science Center, 443-2001
December-January

The Science Center's annual holiday extravaganza features loads of hands-on, educational fun. Held during the winter holiday break, late December through early January.

Chamber Music Play-In

Music Center of the Northwest, 783-2798
Throughout the year

Drop in for an evening of informal chamber music performances by ensembles of all abilities and ages. Play-ins are held two or three times per year, in the fall, winter and summer months. All ages welcome.

Legislature in Session

State Capitol
January-April

Visit Olympia and see our lawmakers in action. See Excursions.

Chinese New Year

Children's Museum, 441-1768
Wing Luke Asian Museum, 623-5124
January

Children can learn about Chinese art and culture and celebrate the New Year in daily hands-on workshops throughout the month of January at the Children's Museum. Wing Luke Asian Museum also has an exhibit every January on Asian New Year Traditions.

Kids and Critters Naturefest

Northwest Trek Wildlife Park, (800) 433-TREK
January

During four days in mid-January, Northwest Trek features special fun and learning about the wildlife in this immense park.

Martin Luther King Jr. Day

Seattle Center House, 684-7200
January

The "Keeping the Dream Alive Celebration" at the Seattle Center provides entertainment, children's activities, speakers and exhibits that commemorate the life of Martin Luther King.

Imagination Celebration

Washington Alliance for Arts Education, 441-4501
January or February

Imagination Celebration features a full week of arts workshops, hands-on activities, exhibits, performances and special events designed for children and teachers exploring arts education. At the Seattle Center.

Whoopteedoo!

Bellevue Parks & Recreation, 451-4106
January-March

This annual performing arts series features the area's best musicians, theatre groups, storytellers, dancers and jugglers at affordable prices.

Weekend of Social Graces

Four Seasons Olympic Hotel, Seattle, 621-1700
January-June

A special weekend-long manners class for children eight-12 years of age, which includes hotel accommodations, meals and an elegant tea party. Children will learn flower arranging, table setting and etiquette, proper introductions, telephone etiquette, social correspondence, finance and overall social savvy. Offered three weekends per year between January and June. One-day mini-seminars are also offered for teens (ages 13-18).

Celebrating African-American History Month

February

Public libraries, community groups, private organizations and others sponsor special events and festivals celebrating African-American History Month each February. The February Festival, Festival Sundiata, and Seattle's Underground Railroad, are just three.

February Festival

Langston Hughes Cultural Arts Center, 684-4757
February

Month-long celebration of African-American history and culture includes talent shows, theatre productions, concerts and exhibits.

Festival Sundiata

Seattle Center, 684-7200
February

Festival celebrating African and African-American cultures, featuring arts and crafts, history, musical performances, and children's activities.

Seattle's Annual Underground Railroad

Consult February's Seattle's Child for details
February

Schools, church organizations, community groups and families are invited to participate in this special annual event featuring training courses and educational tours designed to celebrate the African-American culture.

Northgate Children's Fair

Northgate Shopping Center, 362-4777
February

The North Seattle Community College Parent's Cooperative Preschools present their annual Children's Fair each February at Northgate Shopping Center. This two-day fair features hands-on activities and entertainment for preschool and elementary children, as well as information for parents about cooperative education.

Mini City

Factoria Square, 747-7344
February

The Children's Museum's portable traveling neighborhood visits Factoria Square each February as a fundraiser for Bellevue Community College's Early Childhood Education Program. Lots of hands-on imaginative play in the child-sized railroad station, police car and other settings.

Northwest Flower & Garden Show

224-1700

February

This annual event features demonstrations, exhibits, products and especially hard-to-find plant varieties for sale. Special children's activities include a Children's Garden competition, as well as hands-on activities.

Lake Forest Park Children's Fair

Lake Forest Park Towne Centre, 367-6617

February

A one-day free event with entertainment, storytelling, demonstrations and hands-on creative activities for children.

Smile Day

Seattle Aquarium, Pier 59, 443-7607

February

This annual February event, presented by the Seattle King County Dental Society and held at the Seattle Aquarium, features free dental screenings for children 12 and under. The day is filled with activities, goodies and special guest appearances.

Valentine Train

Lake Whatcom Railway, (206) 595-2218

February

The authentic Lake Whatcom Railway steam train departs Wickersham, 10 miles north of Sedro Woolley on State Highway 9 (about two hours north of Seattle) for a one-hour tour of scenic Whatcom County. The ride features live entertainment, Valentine goodies and fun.

YMCA Run for Kids

Downtown Tacoma YMCA, *(206) 597-6444*

February

Annual event presented by the Downtown Tacoma YMCA, featuring a family walk/run, prizes, drawings and fun! Held in downtown Tacoma each February, it benefits YMCA programs.

Spring

Children's Hospital Health Fair

Children's Hospital and Medical Center, 526-2201
March

This annual fair is designed to help children form positive views about health-care experiences. Includes a tour of an operating room, a hospital play kit, lots of hands-on fun and a hearing screening for ages four years and up.

Irish Week Festival

Seattle Center, 684-7200
March

This annual event features traditional Irish music, singing, dancing, displays, workshops on Irish history and contests to find the child with the reddest hair or the most freckles!

St. Patrick's Day Parade

City Hall to Westlake Center, 623-0340
March

Annual downtown Seattle parade at noon featuring bagpipes, singing, dancing and the laying of a green stripe down the center of Fourth Ave.

Kent Kids Arts Day

Kent Parks & Recreation and Kent Arts Commission, 859-3991
March

A variety of hands-on crafts and entertainment are presented for the younger set.

Redmond Toddler Indoor Carnival

Redmond Parent/Toddler Groups, 869-5605
March

This popular spring carnival is designed for children ages one to five years, and features face painting, cake walks, door prizes, fishing, balloons, hands-on crafts, entertainment and more. Proceeds benefit the Redmond parent/toddler programs.

Whirligig

Seattle Center, 684-7200
March-April

Every Spring, the Seattle Center presents a special month-long indoor carnival, which includes indoor rides, special events, workshops, entertainment and more designed for children ages 10 and under.

Photo credit: Paul Dowling

Sailing on Elliott Bay along the Seattle Waterfront.

Whale Migration

Westport Chamber of Commerce, (206) 268-9422
Island Marina Cruises, Bellingham, (206) 734-8866
March-August

Once the cold weather is on its way out, gray whales return to Alaska from Baja, where they winter and calve. Take a whale-watching excursion to get an unforgetable look at these magnificent creatures.

Daffodil Festival/Grand Floral Street Parade

Daffodil Festival Association, (206) 627-6176
April

The annual Junior Daffodil Parade is designed specifically for children, featuring kids, pets, music and non-motorized floats. Held each year in early April in Tacoma's downtown area. The Grand Floral Street Parade is also held in Tacoma each April and features floats decorated with fresh daffodils, as well as bands, drill teams and clowns.

Puyallup Spring Fair

Puyallup Fairgrounds, (206) 841-5045
April

Carnival rides, a petting farm, livestock shows and the Daffodil Parade.

Kids Fun Fair

KCPQ 13 TV & Linda J. Browne & Assoc., 441-1881
April

Formerly held at the Seattle Center and known as the Child's Fair, this annual event has moved to the Kingdome. The Fair is loaded with information for parents and activities for kids, but has received some unfavorable reviews from parents for long lines and overcrowding.

Seattle Cherry Blossom & Japanese Cultural Festival

Seattle Center, 684-7200
April

Annual festival celebrating the traditional Japanese culture with arts and crafts, tea ceremonies, origami demonstrations and performing arts.

Skagit Valley Tulip Festival

(800) 4-Tulips
April

This annual event features 1500 acres of tulips, irises and daffodils in full bloom, as well as many family activities including arts and crafts, sporting events, pancake breakfasts, bicycling, pony rides and tours aboard the Tulip Transit Vans.

Worldfest

Northgate Shopping Center, 362-477
April

This special two-day spring event celebrates the rich and diverse ethnic communities of the Seattle area with song, dance, arts, crafts and ethnic cuisine. One highlight is the Children of the World Parade, in which children from over 50 nationalities parade in their native costumes.

Seattle Mariners Baseball

Kingdome, 628-3555
April-September

The Seattle Mariners play their season opener in early April and continue through September. Special discounts and promotional events offer fun for the entire family. (See Spectator Sports.)

Tacoma Tigers Baseball

Cheney Stadium, (206) 752-7707
April-September

Tacoma's Class AAA Oakland Athletics Affiliate play baseball outdoors at Cheney Stadium. Promotional activities for families held throughout the season. *(See Spectator Sports.)*

Artspring: A Very Special Arts Festival
Very Special Arts Washington, 443-1843
May

Celebration featuring the visual and performing arts achievements and talents of children and adults with disabilities, as well as interactive hands-on activities and workshops for persons with and without disabilities.

Boating Day
May

Considering there are more small boats per capita in Seattle than in any city in the world, it seems fitting that the first Saturday of every May is set aside for celebrating the opening of boating season. Locals climb into anything that will float and make merry.

The noon parade of decorated boats proceeds eastbound through the Montlake Cut, near the University of Washington. The parade is preceded by crew races beginning at about 10 am. Popular viewing spots include East Montlake Park at the southwest end of the cut and the Lake Washington Ship Canal Trail on the south side. There is also a large deck area at the east end of the cut, easily accessible via a sidewalk at the east end of Shelby Street near the Museum of History and Industry. Get there early for a good view.

Mom and Me at the Zoo
Woodland Park Zoo, 684-4800
Point Defiance Zoo, (206) 591-5337
May

An annual Mother's Day Event held on the Saturday before Mom's Day at Point Defiance and Woodland Park, featuring special activities, entertainment, animal talks and hands-on crafts.

Northwest Folklife Festival
Seattle Center, 684-7300
May

This annual Memorial Day Weekend festival celebrates the Northwest's diverse cultural heritage. The International Children's Village features hands-on activities, workshops and special stage performances just for kids.

Pike Place Market Festival
Pike Place Market, 587-0351
May

Enjoy a variety of entertainment and activities for the entire family on Memorial Day weekend. Don't miss the Kids' Alley, featuring a variety of hands-on activities and entertainment just for kids.

Seattle International Children's Festival

Seattle Center, 684-7346
May

A truly exceptional opportunity to see world-class children's entertainment. Every May, the festival showcases premier children's performers from around the world, including puppeteers, musicians, storytellers, dancing troupes and more. School and community groups attend the weekday performances, but Saturday offers a full day of entertainment for families.

Seattle Maritime Week

Downtown Seattle Association, 623-0340
May

A full week of activities and special events showcasing the maritime industry in the Seattle area. Activities include vessel tours, tugboat races, free admission to many waterfront attractions for kids and more.

University District Street Fair

On University Way, west of the UW campus, 527-2567
May

This granddaddy of Northwest street fairs features 500 booths, music, a children's festival area, an ethnic dance stage and plenty of good people-watching and food.

International Children's Film Festival

Children's Museum, 441-1768
May-June

Highlights children's films from around the world and includes festival-related hands-on activities for children at the theatres prior to each show.

Bicycle Saturdays & Sundays

Seattle Parks & Recreation, 684-8021
May-September

From spring through early fall, Seattle's Department of Parks & Recreation designates one Saturday and Sunday each month as Bicycle Day along Lake Washington Boulevard between Mt. Baker Beach and Seward Park. Free bicycle safety checks and first aid stations are provided along the route, which is closed to motorized vehicles.

Velodrome Bike Racing

Velodrome, Marymoor Park, 389-5825
May-August

A full season of bike racing and events happen from mid-May to early September. *(See Active Play: Outdoor Fun.)*

Summer

Berry Picking

The season for strawberries, raspberries, blueberries and more tasty fruits and veggies begins in June. *(See Harvests for details.)*

Snohomish River Queen

1712 West Marine View Drive, Everett, (206) 259-2743
Year-round

The Snohomish River Queen, a modern replica paddle-wheel steamboat, leaves the Everett Marina for narrated tours of the Marina and Snohomish River Wetlands. Operates year-round, but sailings are most frequent during the summer months. Historic River and Scenic Wildlife Tours are offered, as well as lunch, Sunday brunch, and dinner cruises. Special event cruises include Mother's Day, Easter and Christmas. Reservations are required. (For more information, see Excursions.)

Dad & Me Fun Run

Marymoor Park, Redmond, 344-8709
June

A full day of family fun at the annual Dad & Me Classic Fun Run. Held at Marymoor Park in Redmond, this special event features a 5K competitive run, as well as a Family 5K Walk, a special 1/2-mile course for children six and under, and loads of activities and entertainment. The Fun Run is usually held over Father's Day weekend.

Everett Salty Sea Days

Salty Sea Days Association, (206) 339-1113
June

Annual maritime festival featuring carnival rides, log rolling contests, athletic events, demonstrations, on-going entertainment, celebrity appearances and children's activities.

Fire Festival

Pioneer Square Association, 622-6235
June

Visit Pioneer Square during this June Festival and help your kids learn about the Great Seattle Fire of 1889. Antique fire trucks are on display, and the fire department demonstrates some of its know-how. Good mix of history, entertainment and children's activities.

Photo credit: Roberta Wilkes

Summer berry picking in a field near Seattle.

KidsDay

June

Every year in June, Seattle celebrates kids with one day of entertainment, arts activities and free admission to many popular attractions throughout Seattle, including the Woodland Park Zoo, the Seattle Aquarium, the Monorail, the Center for Wooden Boats, the Children's Museum and more.

Everett Giants Baseball

Everett Memorial Stadium, (206) 258-3673

June-September

An affiliate of the San Francisco Giants, the Everett Giants play outdoor baseball on real grass under real sky. Great family entertainment. (See Spectator Sports.)

Bellevue Jazz Festival

Bellevue Parks Department, 455-6887

July

This annual one- or two-day event gives adult jazz lovers a chance to share their passion for this music form with their kids. The casual set-up, electric energy, and innovative music by local performers makes for a fun and relaxing family day—at a reasonable price. Usually held at either Bellevue Community College or Bellevue Downtown Park.

Kinderfest

Leavenworth Chamber of Commerce, (509) 548-5807
June

A weekend in June dedicated to children, featuring entertainment, activities and hands-on exhibits.

Flight Festival & Air Show

Museum of Flight, 764-5720
July

View a large collection of aircraft, aerobatic performances, hands-on educational programs, live music and other entertainment.

Fourth of July Celebrations

Lots of fun activities for children and families are held throughout the area to celebrate America's birthday, including: activities at Bellevue Downtown Park (451-4106) and in downtown Edmonds (776-6711), Ivar's Fireworks Celebration (587-6500), and the Naturalization Ceremony at the Seattle Center (684-7200).

Kid's Fair

Pacific Northwest Arts & Crafts Fair, 454-4900
July

As part of the popular Pacific Northwest Arts & Crafts Fair held each summer in Bellevue, the Kid's Fair features arts and crafts for kids, by kids and with kids. Lots of hands-on creative and imaginative play.

Lakeshore Curriculum Carnival

Lakeshore Curriculum, 462-8076
July

Annual free carnival for children ages three to nine, featuring arts, crafts, and other hands-on activities.

Marymoor Heritage Festival

Marymoor Park, Redmond, 296-2964
July

Includes local musicians, dancers, arts and crafts demonstrations, foods from around the world, entertainment and a Children's Corner with hands-on activities.

Paine Field International Air Fair

Paine Field, Everett, (206) 355-2266
July

Annual air show featuring military and civilian aircraft, aerobatics, displays, exhibits, music, food and children's activities.

Tivoli—A Bite of Scandinavia

Nordic Heritage Museum, 789-5707
July

An annual family event that features a traditional Swedish pancake breakfast, colorful craft and food booths, musicians, dancers, a full-course salmon barbecue and lots of children's events, games and amusements.

Wooden Boat Festival

Center for Wooden Boats, south end of Lake Union, 382-BOAT
July

Large variety of wooden boats from skiffs to square riggers, on display both in the water and out. Activities include a wooden yacht race, small boat races, working exhibits, music, food, contests and more. Children will enjoy activities designed to teach maritime skills. Usually held over the Fourth of July weekend.

Camlann Medieval Faire

Camlann Medieval Association, (206) 788-1353
Weekends during July and August

Annual Medieval Faire held in Carnation. Special attractions include armored knights in combat, minstrels, dancing, juggling, storytelling and demonstrations in blacksmithing, tile-making, spinning, weaving and candle-making.

Outdoor Concerts

July, August

Many communities throughout the Puget Sound region present outdoor family concerts during July and August, spotlighting a variety of the area's best local talent at little or no cost. Bring a picnic and enjoy the sounds. (See Kid Culture/Music & Variety.)

Seafair Summer Festival

Seafair, 728-0123
July-August

For three weeks during the months of July and August, Seattle and neighboring communities celebrate the Seafair Summer Festival, featuring ethnic/community celebrations and parades, children's parades, sporting events, the U.S. Navy Fleet, the Torchlight Parade, the Unlimited Hydroplane Races and Navy Blue Angels performances. Highlights include the International District Summer Festival, Redmond Derby Days, the Milk Carton Derby on Green Lake and West Seattle's Hi-Yu Festival. Call the Seafair office or your local community group or parks department for a complete schedule of events in your area. The Kiddie parades are especially popular with young audiences.

Bubble Festival
Pacific Science Center, 443-2001
August

Learn everything there is to know about bubbles at Pacific Science Center's popular festival. Attractions include lots of hands-on activities and loads of information on how bubbles are used in everyday life.

Island County Fair
Island County Fairgrounds, Langley, Whidbey Island, (206) 221-4677
August

The Island County Fair is held in Langley each August, with all that a genuine county fair has to offer: hot scones, ferris wheels, displays of the finest produce in the county, logging demonstrations and a first-class parade. On Sunday there is a Barnyard Scramble—small animals and children under seven are turned loose together in a corral. But beware! You may bring a live chicken home with you. What the kids catch, they get to keep!

KOMO Kidsfair
Seattle Center, 684-7200
August

An afternoon of free activities and entertainment for the entire family presented by KOMO Radio and Television and held at the Seattle Center. Attractions include a ride on the KOMO Air 4 Whirlibird, hands-on activities, information and educational exhibits, and visits by television and radio personalities.

Renton River Days
Several sites throughout Renton, 235-2587
August

Nearly a week of family events and entertainment including arts and crafts, art shows, sporting events, a petting zoo for kids, and the popular Yellow Rubber Duck Derby.

Evergreen State Fair
Evergreen Fairgrounds, Monroe, (206) 794-7832
Late August-early September

With all the attractions of a large state fair but on a smaller scale, the Evergreen State Fair features top name entertainment, agricultural exhibits, pig races, clowns, a carnival and lots more.

Fall

Bumbershoot
Seattle Center, 682-4386
September

Held each year over the Labor Day weekend, Bumbershoot, the Seattle Arts Festival, presents a full line-up of family entertainment, including top-rate live music, art exhibits, food, theatre, arts and crafts and more.

Fiestas Patrias
Seattle Center, 684-7200
September

Held every September in celebration of Mexican and Latin American independence, featuring dancing, music, crafts, ethnic foods and exhibits.

Puyallup Fair
Puyallup Fairgrounds, (206) 841-5045
September

The sixth largest fair in the United States, featuring a wide variety of family events and activities. Top-name entertainment, petting farm, farm animals, home crafts, carnival rides, agricultural displays and food, food, food (a bag of hot raspberry scones is a must)! Metro buses (553-3000) provide excellent direct service right to the fairgrounds, a good way to avoid the parking and traffic hassles.

St. Demetrios Greek Festival
St. Demetrios Greek Orthodox Church, 325-4347
September

Authentic Greek food, arts and crafts, games for children, folk dancing and entertainment offered for one weekend in September. Very popular.

Wallingford Wurst Festival
St. Benedict School, 633-3375
September

Annual free festival includes children's games, carnival rides, live entertainment, international food, dancers, music and more.

Woodinville Family Fun Festival
Woodinville Chamber of Commerce, 481-8300
September

This annual free festival features canoe races, a family fun run/walk, a salmon barbecue, entertainment, police and fire vehicle displays, and more.

Photo credit: The Herbfarm

Leavenworth Autumn Leaf Festival

Leavenworth Chamber of Commerce, (509) 548-5807

Last weekend of September

Celebrates the splendor of fall foliage with a parade, food, Bavarian music and hands-on activities for kids.

Halloween Fun and Pumpkin Picking

Communities throughout the Puget Sound area offer a variety of Halloween activities for children of all ages. Check local parks departments, Camp Long in West Seattle, Pacific Science Center, local shopping malls and Northwest Trek for details about special programs.

Also, many farms just outside the city have pumpkin patches where your children can pick their own jack-o-lanterns straight off the vine. (See Harvests.)

Festa Italiana

Seattle Center, 684-7200

October

Music, dancing and food in celebration of the Italian culture.

King County Library Used Book Sale

684-6605

October

Great deals on furniture, children's books, records and cassettes.

Issaquah Salmon Days

Downtown Issaquah, 392-0661
October

This annual weekend festival, celebrating the return of the salmon up Issaquah Creek, features a parade, arts and crafts, children's activities, continuous entertainment, food and more.

Molbak's Fairyland

Molbak's Greenhouse and Nursery, Woodinville, 483-5000
October

Each October, Molbak's is transformed into a floral fairyland with scenes that recreate a favorite children's story. Local theatre groups perform dramatizations of the story; families are invited to drop in, browse and enjoy the displays.

Discover Music!

Seattle Symphony, 443-4747
October-March

Each year, the Seattle Symphony presents a special series of musical performances designed to introduce children ages six to 10 years to the world of classical music.

Sandy Bradley Live Radio Show

October-May

Live radio show broadcasts each Saturday morning, October through May, from the Museum of History and Industry. Fun entertainment for kids on a rainy weekend. (See Kid Culture/Music & Variety.)

RESTAURANTS

CHAPTER 8

Basics

SHOPPING

LIST

ESSENTIALS

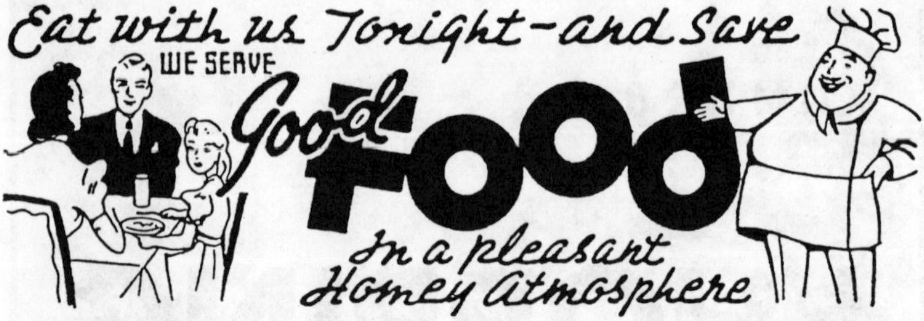

Restaurants

Following, you'll find a list of good places in Seattle to take kids to eat. These are not the restaurants where mom nibbles wild greens while junior sucks silently on pasta *al burro*. We are talking serious family eateries here—where your toddler can fling a fistful of rice without shaming you out of the place, the highchairs aren't quaint antiques that can be flipped over with one good arch of the back, and the food and service are worth the effort and money.

It's hard to have a good dining-out experience with a young eater, and when a grown-up is brave or foolish enough to venture into a restaurant with a child, we believe they deserve all the good food and helpful service they can possibly get. This list was compiled from our own experiences as parents and from the recommendations of fellow parents. The selections were made with the following criteria in mind:

Good Food. For the adults and the kids.
Kid Friendly. You and your kids should feel genuinely welcome, even if your kids don't always act like short British diplomats. Your waitperson will hopefully distract a fussy baby and cheerfully clean up spilled milk, instead of glowering unsympathetically as the behavior at your table begins to deteriorate.
Fair Prices: A typical kid goes through numerous eating stages, ranging from nibbling two bites per meal to inhaling everything in sight and still feeling "starved." Both phases are costly if you are eating out. The period between these two extremes seems to occupy a very small window of time, so the prices for kids' meals should give parents a break.
Fast Service. Most young kids sitting in a restaurant are time bombs waiting to blow. In everyone's interest, your wait person should go for top efficiency, recognizing you are here to refuel and leave, not to linger over meaningful conversation. We don't think any meal is worth a long wait when you are dining with kids.
Entertainment. This is not essential for placement on our list, but it does give the adults that extra two minutes to gulp down their meals. A floor show is not necessary, but it sure helps to offer a cup of crayons or a balloon.

A. Jay's

2619 1st Ave, Downtown Seattle
441-1511
Breakfast, lunch every day
1320 Madison St; Madison Park
328-3993
Breakfast, lunch every day, dinner Mon-Fri

A full deli menu served with speed and generous proportions. Like most delicatessens, the selection is varied enough to satisfy the widely divergent tastes found in a mixed group of adults and kids. The bagel with cream cheese will suit most four-year-olds; the omelets, corned beef and french toast are highly recommended for the adults. The pancakes may be the lightest (and biggest) in town—one order will easily serve a dad and his preschooler. Two kids can split a half-order (one pancake) and still walk out stuffed.

Alki Homestead

2717 61st SW, West Seattle
935-5678
Dinner every day except Mon & Tues

There is a very narrow slice of the population that is perfectly suited for this old-fashioned restaurant: little girls, ages five-10, who are charmed by old-fashioned elegance. They will be enchanted while everybody else has an okay dining experience. Located in a genuine log cabin (built in 1904) and decked out with lace tablecloths and fine crystal, it is not a place to take preschoolers. The specialty of the house is pan-fried chicken dinner with all the fixings ($10.95). This is an ideal restaurant for a night on the town with one child, not a feeding stop for a hungry brood. Reservations required.

Azteca

Seattle: Lake Union, University Village, Northgate area, Shilshole and Ballard
Eastside: Bellevue, Eastgate, Totem Lake
Lunch, dinner every day

Azteca does an outstanding job of serving good Mexican food quickly and at reasonable prices. Children are made to feel welcome by the gracious attitude of the staff, an excellent children's menu, and crayons and balloons. The prices are good every day (regular entrees $5-$10, a child's meal from the children's menu is $2.95), but Sundays are an even better deal for families, when a child's meal is only $.95!

Blue Star Cafe and Pub

4512 Stone Way N, Seattle
548-0345
Dinner every day, weekends lunch & dinner

Granted it is called a pub and there are no crayons or other kid atttractions provided, but this new, spacious spot at the west end of Wallingford (across from McDonald's) has such fast service you probably won't need anything to entertain your kids. There's a good standard children's menu, featuring reasonably priced, generously dished helpings (fettuccine at $3.50 is the top dollar item). Older kids with big appetites will find a good selection on the regular menu since the theme of the place is home-style cooking. There is plenty of elbow room and the cheerful hum of folks having a good time, so you won't feel conspicuous if your kids get wiggly while you savor the last morsels of your delicious meal.

Capons Rotisserie Chicken

1815 N 45th St, Seattle
547-3949
605 15th Ave E, Seattle
323-4026
Lunch, dinner every day

The only requirement for a successful meal at this cheerful, cafeteria-style spot is that everybody likes chicken because chicken is all they serve—along with a choice of tasty stuffing, mashed potatoes, vegetables and salads. Prices are reasonable—half a chicken for $5.30, a quarter bird for $4.55—with your choice of two side dishes and a corn bread muffin. The rotisserie roasted chicken is fall-off-the-bone, finger licking good. The side dishes can be ordered alone; creamy mashed potatoes ($1.95) make a dandy meal for a toddler. Chicken sandwiches, chicken soup and chicken pot pies are also served. Good for take-out, too.

Chinooks

1900 W Nickerson St, Seattle
283-4665
Lunch, dinner every day, breakfast Sat-Sun

There is plenty for kids to look at through the large windows that enclose this big, bustling restaurant on Fisherman's Terminal near Ballard. The view of the working

marina will provide diversion and the wide selection of good food (over 125 items on dinner menu plus daily specials) will delight the adults. This is a good place to bring the out-of-town relatives—they'll get a flavor for the boat life of Seattle and the chance to eat well-prepared seafood, and you won't get wiped-out by the check. (Dinner entrees $7.95-$14.95.) There is often a short wait for breakfast on the weekends, but kids can easily be distracted by a walk among the hundreds of fishing boats. Once you are seated, a basket of scrumptious fresh-baked scones will arrive at your table, along with orange butter. If you want to work off your meal afterwards, drive a few blocks west to Discovery Park, the largest park in the city (see Discovery Park in the Parks chapter).

Cucina!Cucina!

901 Fairview, Seattle
447-2782
800 Bellevue Way, Bellevue
637-1177
17770 Southcenter Pkwy, Tukwila
575-0520)
Lunch, dinner every day

Upon entering Cucina!Cucina! your child is offered a balloon—an instant hit. Crayons and a color-in menu follow, and if that isn't enough, your table is covered with white butcher paper, so that the coloring can extend onto the table or you can start a round of tic-tac-toe. The child's menu offers individual pizza ($2.95 includes milk or soda) and a good selection of pasta dishes, such as plain buttered pasta and spaghetti with meatballs. The smell of garlicy foccacia and fresh sourdough bread fill the place but be forewarned — a basket of bread costs $3. (Complimentary bread is a sorely missed item when you are a parent with a kid on the verge of a hunger breakdown and a surprising oversight for a restaurant catering to kids.)

The decor at the Seattle location is festive and playful, enlivened by the activity on Lake Union visible out the windows. You won't dine on the finest Italian cuisine in town, but you will eat decent and sometimes inspired food at moderate prices and your kids will probably come away feeling they have had a fun treat.

Green Village

721 S King St, Seattle
624-3634
Lunch, dinner every day except Tues

Green Village 2

514 6th Ave S, Seattle
621-1719
Lunch, dinner every day except Sun

At Green Village on S King your toughest moment will be choosing from the menu of over 100 items. Don't agonize too much though; we haven't found a bad choice yet. The style is mostly Szechwan and curry, so you will need to be careful to not order foods that will be too hot for young palettes. All the noodle dishes are wonderful; the seafood dishes are also exceptional (however, stay away from the seafood if you are dining on a tight budget). There are several big round tables that can comfortably seat eight so this is a fine place to come with a big group.

If you hanker for Chinese food but you want a quicker and less expensive alternative, head down to Green Village 2. This little hole-in-the-wall has a very limited menu (House Special Rice Noodles, $4.50 with soup; Three Types of Seafood Noodles, $4.95; Vegetables Over Rice, $4.25). There are no high chairs at Green Village 2. After your meal, walk across the street to browse in Uwajimaya (see In & Around Downtown/International District).

Iron Horse

311 3rd Ave S, Pioneer Square
233-9506
Lunch, dinner every day

We break a few of our own standards by including this place—like rule number one: the food must be good. The food is not bad here, just mediocre. But go anyway, because every child deserves to have the experience of getting his hamburger delivered by a toy train. A toot of the whistle announces your order is on its way, and when you see your preschooler's face as the train pulls up at her table, you'll be glad you came. Fare is standard—salads, burgers, sandwiches at moderate prices; train paraphernalia covers the walls. This is also a good place to have a birthday party (the train delivers the birthday cake). Call to order a cake ($9) and reserve a table for such an occasion.

Ivar's Acres of Clams

Pier 54, Seattle
624-6852
Lunch, dinner every day

Ivar's Indian Salmon House

401 Northlake Way, Seattle
632-0767
Lunch Mon-Fri; brunch Sun ;dinner every day

Ivar's Mukilteo Landing

710 Front St, Mukilteo
347-3648
Lunch, dinner every day

With a children's menu that doubles as a colorful mask, friendly waitpersons who go out of their way to make kids feel welcome, and good food at very reasonable prices (salmon, cornbread and slaw for $6.75), Ivar's is a quintessential family restaurant. All three restaurants have the added attraction of being located on the water, so there's always a good view of the boat activity. All three restaurants also have a take-out counter outside — a great option on a summer night.

Our favorite of the three is the Indian Salmon House. The setting is a replica of an Indian longhouse, with magnificent canoes, masks and photographs decorating the dining area. Cod and salmon are cooked over a smoky alder fire—kids enjoy watching the cooks working over the big fire. This is an ideal place to take an out-of-town family to give them a glimpse of Northwest Indian culture along with a good salmon meal and a water view.

King's Table Buffet

1545 NW Market, Seattle
784-8955
2222 California SW, West Seattle
937-2999
12120 NE 85th, Kirkland
828-3811

O.K. fine—go ahead and scoff. You are positive you'll never darken the doors. But wait until you're feeding a batch of school-age kids with hollow legs or a toddler that likes to throw food instead of eat it. All of a sudden the no-wait, all-you-can-eat features will be more appealing than any four-star restaurant's comforts. And though the food may not be quite as palatable, it is ideal for children's tastes: jello, mashed potatoes, spaghetti, macaroni, roast beef, etc. A parent can eat well on the salad bar and the fabulous fried chicken. Everyone will be content making his or her own ice cream sundae for dessert. Best of all, the prices show refreshing logic—the older the kid the more you pay. Adults pay $6.99; kids under 12 pay $0.45 per year of age (a five-year-old pays 5 X $0.45= $2.25). Thursday nights are family nights; kids eat for $0.39 per year.

Luna Park Cafe

2918 SW Avalon Way, West Seattle
935-7250
Breakfast, lunch, dinner every day

Jukeboxes all over the place (the owner also owns a jukebox store), a batmobile right in the joint, a genuine soda fountain serving up thick creamy milkshakes and an extensive child's menu that includes Mickey Mouse pancakes and cowabunga burgers — West Seattle is not that far away. And if taking your kids to groove on the '50s decor isn't enough to get you there, the tasty, down-home food (turkey sandwich, spinach salad, meatloaf and potatoes, etc.) should be.

(Take Spokane St exit, then the Harbor Ave exit. Turn left onto S Avalon; the restuarant is on your right.)

Market Cafe at the Westin Hotel

1900 5th, in the Westin Hotel
728-1000
Breakfast, lunch, dinner everyday

It is surprisingly difficult to find a good meal in downtown Seattle that will satisfy both adults and children while not breaking the budget. At this cheery cafe located off the main lobby of the Westin Hotel (close to the monorail station) you and your child will find a wide variety of healthy and delicious choices and a kitchen that is exceptionally accomodating to the finicky eater. Crayons are provided and service is excellent. This is a good place to take a child before a night out at the theatre.

The Old Spaghetti Factory

2801 Elliott Ave
441-7724
Lunch, dinner every day

The first clue that this place is good for families is its name: "Factory" is not a word usually associated with elegant dining. Even so, the Spaghetti Factory has managed to create a festive atmosphere, with Victorian style decor, a beautiful old weighing scale (only kids love to weigh themselves before and after dinner), and a real caboose that sits in the middle of the main dining area (good luck waiting for one of its few tables). What *is* factory-like is the speed and efficiency of the wait staff and the sheer size of the place.

The food is delicious and very reasonably priced (spaghetti with clam sauce, $5.35; Meatballs and spaghetti, $6.25; combo plate of meat sauce, mushroom sauce and Mistrathara cheese, $5.95). All dinners include salad, a loaf of sourdough bread (served with plain and garlic butters) and spumoni for dessert. Kids get a paper train conductor's cap and a choice of special meals that come on plastic dinosaur plates (so popular they will sell you the dinner sets). A popular young kiddie meal includes spaghetti with tomato sauce, applesauce, beverage, dinosaur cookie and frozen treat for $2.95 ($3.35 with a meatball; $3.95 for lasagna instead of spaghetti). A junior meal, for bigger or hungrier children costs $3.75 and includes spaghetti, salad, bread, beverage and spumoni. Since you aren't the only parent in town looking for good food and service at a great price in a fun setting, plan to go early (before 5:30 pm) if you want to avoid a wait. Reservations not accepted.

Thai Palace

2224 8th Ave
343-7846
Lunch, dinner every day

There are so many good Thai restaurants in this area, it is hard to recommend one over the others. This is our favorite because the food is always exceptionally good, the prices are moderate and the dining room large, light and rarely crowded. Kids love the spring rolls and Phad Thai noodles (order with "no stars" or it will be too spicy for young eaters); adults rave about the Seafood Potuen and Sizzling Cod.

Shopping List

The Greater Seattle area offers an exceptionally diverse assortment of toy, clothing, book and furniture stores that specialize in products for children. Here are some of the best:

On the Eastside

CLOTHING

Benetton 0-12
Bellevue Square, Bellevue
451-7300

Bon Marche
Bellevue Square, Bellevue
455-2121

Brat Pack
16564 Cleveland St, Ste P, Redmond
883-1006

European Child
125 Central Way, Kirkland
827-2012

GapKids
Bellevue Square, Bellevue
454-1539

Gymboree
Bellevue Square, Bellevue
450-9460

Kid's Club
15600 NE 8th
Crossroads Shopping Ctr, Bellevue
643-KIDS

Nordstrom
Bellevue Square, Bellevue
455-5800

Offspring Ltd.
1490 NW Gilman Blvd
Meadows Shopping Ctr, Issaquah
391-7780

Parkplace Kids
224 Parkplace Ctr, Kirkland
828-8904

Sprouts
Gilman Village, Issaquah
392-2049

SHOES

The Shoe Zoo
240 NW Gilman Blvd, Issaquah
392-8211

Stride Rite
Bellevue Square, Bellevue
453-0101

CONSIGNMENT CLOTHING AND TOYS

Kids Kingdom
15525 Main St, Duvall
788-2938

Poppets Pre-Loved Clothing
149 Front St N, Issaquah
557-0081

Play It Again Toys
16003 Redmond Way, Redmond
881-6920

The Mouse Closet
521 156th Ave SE, Bellevue
641-0531

The Tree House
15742 Redmond Way, Redmond
885-1145

Twinkle Twinkle Little Store
13804 NE 175th, Woodinville
483-8914

TOYS

Imaginarium
Bellevue Square, Bellevue
453-5288

Imagination Express
1175 NW Gilman Blvd, Issaquah
392-3847

Learning World
Bellevue Square, Bellevue
455-1995

Pinnochio's Toys
320 Kirkland Park Place, Kirkland
827-1100

Play Co. Toys
Gilman Village, Issaquah
392-7448

Thinker Toys
10680 NE 8th St, Bellevue
453-0051

BOOKSTORES

All For Kids Books & Music
170 Front St N, Issaquah
391-4089

Island Books
3014 78th Ave SE, Mercer Island
232-6920

Little Professor Book Store
612 228th Ave NE, Redmond, on the Redmond Plateau
391-0669 or 868-7894

Main Street Kids Book Company
10217 Main St, Bellevue
455-8814

Puss 'n Books
15788 Redmond Way, Redmond
885-6828

University Bookstore
990 102nd Ave NE, Bellevue
646-3300

CHILDREN'S FURNITURE

A Child's Room
15123 NE 24th St, Redmond
643-7050

Bellini's
201 Bellevue Way NE, Bellevue
451-0126

Go To Your Room
13000 Bel-Red Rd, Bellevue
453-2990

Kids' Castle
4092 Factoria Square SE, Bellevue
641-4460

Kids Corner
Gilman Village, Issaquah
557-8697

Precious Places
1075 Bellevue Way NE #142, Bellevue
635-7442

MATERNITY

Baby Love Maternity
Bellevue Square, Bellevue
454-2122

Maternity Factory Outlet
141 Park Lane, Kirkland
827-7062

Motherhood Maternity
Bellevue Square, Belleuve
454-1355

Women's Work Maternity
11010 NE 8th, Bellevue
451-1945

Downtown Seattle

CLOTHING

Alley Kids
1904 Post Alley, Pike Place Market
728-0609

Bon Marche
1601 3rd Ave
344-2121

Boston Street Baby
101 Stewart St
728-1490

KidGear
1420 5th Ave
Pacific First Center
624-0756

Nordstrom
1501 5th Ave
628-2111

TOYS

Reminiscence
400 Pine St
Westlake Center
623-6825

City Kites/City Toys
1501 Western Ave
622-5349

Emerald Earth Toys
1530 Post Alley, Pike Place Market
447-9566

Great Wind Kite Shop
402 Occidental Ave S, Pioneer Square
624-6886

Learning World
500 Westlake N
464-1515

Magic Mouse Toys
603 1st Ave
682-8097

The Nature Company
2001 Western Ave
443-1608

Toytropolis
Bon Marche (downtown only)
1601 3rd Ave
344-8916

BOOKSTORES

Brentano's Bookstore
Westlake Center
467-9626

Elliott Bay Book Company
101 S Main, Pioneer Square
624-6600

MATERNITY

Fifth Avenue Maternity
415 Pike St
343-9470

Womens Work Maternity
1522 5th Ave
343-7937

University/Wallingford/ Fremont/Greenwood

CLOTHING

B.G.T. University Sports
University Village Mall
527-1169

Boston St. Baby Store
1815 N 45th St
728-1490

Fine Threads
University Village Mall
525-5888

Me 'n Moms
1021 NE 65th St
524-9344

Sprouts
University Village Mall
524-2553

SHOES

The Shoe Zoo
University Village Mall
525-2770

CONSIGNMENT CLOTHES AND BOOKS

Kid's On 45th
1720 N 45th S
633-KIDS (5437)

TOYS

Kid's Kraft
1711 N 45th (near Wallingford Ctr)
632-5160

Imagination Toys
1815 N 45th St
Wallingford Center, Seattle
547-2356

Teri's Toybox
University Village Mall
526-7147

Top Ten Toys
104 N 85th St
782-0098

BOOKSTORES

All for Kids Books & Music
2943 NE Blakeley
526-2768

Fremont Place Book Company
621 N 35th St
547-5970

Kay's Bookmark
University Village Mall
522-3989

Killing Time Mystery Books
2821 NE 55th St
525-2266

Secret Garden Children's Bookshop
7900 E Green Lake Dr N
524-4556

University Book Store
4326 University Way NE
634-3400

FURNITURE
Go To Your Room
6411 12th Ave NE
Roosevelt Square
528-0711

MATERNITY
Village Maternity
University Village Mall
523-5167

Queen Anne/Magnolia

CLOTHING
Cótton Caboodle
203 W Thomas
285-0075

Small Fry
3214 W McGraw
283-4556

CONSIGNMENT CLOTHING AND TOYS
Outgrown Treasures
3311-A W McGraw, Seattle
285-1809

Madison Valley/ Madison Park

CLOTHING
Kids in the Park
4105 E Madison
324-0449

CONSIGNMENT CLOTHING
A to Z Children's Consignment
2812-111 E Madison St
325-9903

BOOKSTORES
Madison Park Books
4105 E Madison
328-READ

South

CLOTHING
Bon Marche
Southcenter Mall, Tukwila
575-2121

Nordstrom
Southcenter Mall, Tukwila
246-0400

Sweet Pea Boutique
10612 Kent-Kangley Rd SE #101, Kent
859-0202

TOYS
Imaginarium
Southcenter Mall, Tukwila
439-8980

BOOKSTORES
Children's Bookshop
303 West Meeker, Kent
852-0383

FURNITURE
Kids' Castle
17312 Southcenter Parkway, Tukwila
575-2750

North

CLOTHING
Bel Enfant
16611 93rd St SE, Snohomish
800-358-6666

Bon Marche
Northgate Mall, Seattle
361-2121
Alderwood Mall, Lynnwood
771-2121

Burlington Coat Factory
Hwy 99, Edmonds
776-2221

Nordstrom
Northgate Mall, Seattle
364-8800
Alderwood Mall, Lynnwood
771-5755, 233-5351 (from Seattle)

Yvonne's Corner for Kids
422 Main St, Edmonds
778-7600

SHOES

Stride Rite
Northgate Mall, Seattle
364-7920
Alderwood Mall, Lynnwood
771-8434

CONSIGNMENT CLOTHING AND TOYS

About Face Consignment
7300 196th St SW, Lynnwood
771-4190

Just For You
1114 N 183rd St, Seattle
542-3993

Kym's Kiddie Corner
11721 15th Ave NE, Seattle
361-5974

Saturday's Child
18012 Bothell-Everett Hwy, Bothell
(206) 486-6716

TOYS

Bearadise
10416 Aurora Ave N, Seattle
524-1870

Imaginarium
Alderwood Mall, Lynnwood
771-7220

Learning World
TJ Maxx Plaza, Lynnwood
771-4151

Teri's Toybox
526 Main St, Edmonds
774-3190

Tree Top Toys
Lake Forest Park Towne Ctr, Seattle
363-5460

BOOKSTORES

Fireside Book Company
17171 Bothell Way NE, Lake Forest Park Towne Centre, Seattle
364-2298

Tiger Tales Children's Books
420 5th Ave S, Edmonds
775-7405

FURNITURE

Burlington Coat Factory
Hwy 99, Edmonds
776-2221

COSTUMES, PARTY STUFF

Display & Costume
11201 Roosevelt Way NE, Seattle
362-4810
4835 Evergreen Way, Everett
259-2854

Essentials

Transportation

Metro Bus Transit

Throughout King County
553-3000
Buses operate daily
Fares: one zone, $.85-$1.10/adults; two zone, $1.10-$1.60/adults; $.75/ children ages 5-17 (anywhere in King County); children under 5 are free (up to four children with one adult)

Getting there can be as much fun as the destination itself if you let Metro do the driving within King County. Just call 553-3000 and tell the Metro representative where you are and where you want to go, and they'll give you all the information you need: where to catch the bus at what time, where to transfer if necessary, what time you'll arrive at your destination, and how much the ride will cost. Rates vary depending on the time of day; fares are higher during rush hour. Rides in the downtown business district between Jackson and Battery streets and the Waterfront and 6th Avenue are free all day, which makes travel between Pioneer Square, the International District, Pike Place Market, Westlake Mall, the shopping district, and the Waterfront a cheap thrill. You may also board from the Downtown Transit Tunnel at 5th & Jackson, University Street, Westlake Mall and Convention Place and enjoy a free tour beneath the streets of Seattle. Subterranean attractions include a clock made out of tools, neon art and ornate iron work.

Metro also offers monthly passes and ticket books for frequent riders, as well as special Saturday and Sunday passes. If you already know where you board the bus, ask the Metro representative about Bus Time, an automated system with recorded information offering the next two or three departure times for your particular route. For Sunday or holiday travel, a Family Pass is available, which entitles the entire family to ride anywhere in King County all day for $1.70 per adult (two children under 17 years, plus up to four children under 5 years are included with each paying adult fare). These passes can be purchased from the driver as you board the bus.

Monorail

Runs between Seattle Center House & Westlake Center
684-7200
Winter hours: Sun-Thurs, 9 am-9 pm; Fri-Sat, 9 am-midnight
Summer hours (mid-June through Labor Day): daily, 9 am-midnight
One way fare: $.80/adults, $.60/ children ages 5-12, $.25/seniors and disabled persons, children under five are free

Constructed for the 1962 World's Fair, the Monorail seats about 122 people and offers an elevated view of the downtown area, as well as convenient travel between two of the most popular areas in the city: the shopping district and the Seattle Center grounds. Board the monorail from either the third floor of Westlake Center or in the Center's Fun Forest. The trip takes just under two minutes and runs about every 15 minutes throughout the day (more often during the lunch hour).

Washington State Ferries

464-6400 or (800) 843-3779
Operate year-round
Schedules & rates vary for each route

Operating the largest ferry system in the United States, the Washington State Ferries system connects island and peninsula communities throughout the Puget Sound region. Passengers can ride aboard a variety of boats within the fleet, from the smallest passenger-only ferry, which carries 250 people, to the jumbo ferry, which carries 2,000 people and 206 cars. The passenger-only ferry is used for the downtown Seattle to Vashon Island and Seattle to Bremerton runs; the jumbo ferries are used for the Seattle to Bainbridge Island run. The shortest ride is from Fauntleroy to Vashon Island (some riders have reported eagle and whale sightings on this run). The longest ride is from Seattle to Bremerton, which lasts just about one hour. One of the more interesting runs is the Keystone run, which takes you from Whidbey Island to Port Townsend—one of the most charming communities in the Puget Sound area.

Passengers are welcome to bring their own food on board, or enjoy something from the cafeteria. There is a children's meal offered, much like the popular Happy Meal from McDonald's, packaged in a 'ferry box' to take home. Also, though the ferry system does not organize or schedule birthdays, nothing prohibits people from having such a celebration on board.

Waterfront Streetcar

553-3000
Fares: non-rush hour, $.85/adults; rush-hour, $1.10/adults; $.75/children ages 5-17 (all hours); children under five are free
Operates daily year-round every 20-30 minutes; seasonal hours vary

Metro's bright green Waterfront Streetcar travels between Pier 70 and the International District, with nine stops along the way. The route follows the scenic Seattle Waterfront on Alaskan Way to Main Street, through Pioneer Square to 5th & South Jackson St. If you plan to get off the streetcar and then on again within an hour, ask the conductor for a transfer, which will allow you to board another streetcar along the way without paying additional fares. The conductors offer information on what sites are located at each stop, and can offer assistance to help you find your destination.

Resources

Seattle's Child, Eastside Parent and Pierce County Parent monthly newsmagazines
2107 Elliott Ave, Suite 303, Seattle, WA 98121
441-0191

Available for free at several family-oriented businesses or by subscription, *Seattle's Child, Eastside Parent* and *Pierce County Parent* are the best local sources for what to do and where to go with children. Regular features include a monthly calendar of events for children, detailed activity listings, book and restaurant reviews, and health news. Articles address a wide range of issues that affect families. Several supplements are published throughout the year, including *A New Arrival* in February and August (for new and expectant parents); *Summer Learning* in April (summer classes and activities for kids); the *Family Phone Book* in July (services, stores and resources for families); the *Education Directory* in November (elementary, junior high and high schools—public, private and special needs); the *After-School Activity Guide* in September; and the *A to Z Holiday Buying Guide* in December. To pick up a complimentary copy or start a subscription, call 441-0191 or send in the form at the back of this book.

Public Libraries

King County Public Libraries: 462-9600 or 1-800-462-9600
Pierce County Public Libraries: 536-6500
Seattle Public Libraries: 386-4636
Sno-Isle (Snohomish/Island County) Libraries: 1-800-342-1936
Tacoma Public Libraries: 591-5666
Hours vary

Your local public library is not just a place for research and study—it's a family resource, with events and activities for every member of your family. In addition to loaning out books, audio cassettes and videos, the library systems offer a wide variety of programs, including on-going preschool storytimes and parenting programs, hands-on science programs, craft activities, concerts, author appearances, used book sales, and family movies. Contact your local library for their complete schedule of events. Most libraries have a children's librarian available to answer questions about the programs and to help children in their reading selections.

Note: If your child wants a story and you just can't oblige, let them "Dial a Story," at 386-4656.

Hot Lines

Emergency (24 hours a day): 911
Washington Poison Center (24 hours a day): 526-2121 or 800-732-6985
Children's Resource Line (7 am-11 pm daily, for questions about your child's growth, development and health): 526-2500

Little Helpers

A handful of local theatres have crying rooms—glassed-in areas where the kids can do some primal therapy without disrupting all the other families at the cinema.

- *Guild St. Theatre, 2115 N 45th St, 633-3353*
- *Varsity Theatre, 4329 NE University Way, 632-3131*
- *Metro Cinemas, 4500 Ninth Ave NE, 633-0055*
- *Northgate Theatre, 10 Northgate Plaza, 363-5800*

Most of these crying rooms are small (the exception being Northgate's). The Guild, Varsity and Metro are multi-feature movie houses, so call before going to make sure that the feature you wish to see is being shown in the crying room.

Quick Index

Birthday Party Ideas

Birthday Party Packages

Birthday Present Shopping

See also Basics/Shopping List

Classes

Field Trips

Food Places

See also Basics/Restaurants

Free Fun

Children's Corner Radio
Concerts in the Park
Daybreak Star Center
Farmers Markets
Henry Art Gallery (free Thurs)
The Herbfarm
Hiram M. Chittenden Government Locks
Issaquah Alps Trail Club
Kelsey Creek Community Park/Farm
KidStar Radio
Klondike Gold Rush National Historical Park
Nordic Heritage Museum (free first Tues of every month)
Pacific Arts Center
Parks
Seattle Art Museum (free first Tues of every month)
Seattle Chamber Music Festival (outside on the lawn)
Snoqualmie Falls Park
Tacoma Art Museum (every Tues)

Good Beachcombing

Alki Beach
Discovery Park
Golden Gardens
Lincoln Park

Good Family Outing on a Summer Night

Camp Long Overnight Cabins
Discovery Park Night Walks
Everett Giants
Howl-Ins (Wolf Haven)
Seattle Chamber Music Festival: Under the Stars
Seattle Mariners
University Of Washington Observatory
Woodland Park Zoo Outdoor Concerts

Good Family Outing on a Winter Night

Ice Skating
Indoor Family Entertainment Centers
Indoor Playgrounds
Roller Skating
Swimming (Indoor Pools)
Theatres
University of Washington Husky Basketball

Good Places to Fly a Kite

Discovery Park
Gas Works Park
Magnuson Park
Marymoor Park

Good Swimming Beaches

Coulon Park
Green Lake
Lake Sammamish State Park
Luther Burbank Park
Magnuson Park
Matthew's Beach
Meydenbauer Park
Newcastle Beach
Saltwater State Park
Seward Park

Good Walking

Bellefield Nature Park
Camp Long
Discovery Park
Issaquah Alps Trail Club
Marymoor Park
The Mountaineers
St. Edward State Park
Seward Park
Washington Park Arboretum

Recommended for Middle Years (Ages 9-13)

Biking
Boating
Boeing Tour Center
Everett Giants
Fishing
Fun Forest
Geology Adventures

Recommended for Preschoolers

Open on Christmas Day

Public Art Fun for Kids

Index

R

S

T

U

Fundraising

Raise money for your school or organization with books from Northwest Parent Publishing.

Schools, clubs, employee groups and other organizations can raise funds by selling the books published by Northwest Parent Publishing.

Call (206) 441-0191 for information about fundraising opportunities or write to:

Northwest Parent Publishing, Inc.
2107 Elliott Ave, Suite 303
Seattle, WA 98121

Out and About Seattle with Kids notes

We are interested in your comments on using this guide. Did we give you the information you needed? Did you have a terrific experience at one of the places we suggested? Or a disaster? Also, tell us about any places you felt were left out. Give us the details!

Your name Lindsey Brodie

Address 19645 65th Ave NE

City/State/Zip Seattle, WA 98155

Phone (206) 481-2078

Mail to: Northwest Parent Publishing, Inc.
2107 Elliott Ave, Suite 303, Seattle WA 98121